PARROTS

A
COMPLETE
GUIDE

PARROTS

A
COMPLETE
GUIDE

ROSEMARY LOW

MEREHURST

LONDON

Published 1988 by Merehurst Press
Merehurst Limited
Ferry House
51-57 Lacy Road
Putney
London SW15 1PR

© Copyright 1988 Merehurst Limited
ISBN 1 85391 184 4

Editor: Lesley Young
Designer: Carole Perks
Typesetting by Deltatype Ltd, Ellesmere Port, UK
Reprographics by J Film Process Ltd, Bangkok, Thailand
Printed in Portugal by Printer Portuguesa Industria Grafica LDA

ACKNOWLEDGEMENTS

Almost all the photographs in this book are by Rosemary Low and depict birds at the Loro Parque zoological park in Tenerife, of which she is the Curator. The Author wishes to acknowledge the help of Sandra Mason and Inmaculada Mendez at Loro Parque, without whose patience in holding the chicks, photographs of young birds would have been impossible.

Other photographs inside the book are by courtesy of Ardea London/Graham Chapman (page 68), Dennis Avon (88, 106), *Cage and Aviary Birds* magazine (48, 70, 131) and Robin Williams (66).

CONTENTS

Foreword

Ernest Hemingway's pet parrot still sits on a perch in a bar in Barcelona – old, wise, enigmatic and given to uttering an occasional salty epithet; the epitome of this unique and intriguing family of birds.

Parrots are different from other birds, not just in any physical respect or by dint of their high intelligence, but in their attitude to *Homo sapiens*. These birds that can, as Shakespeare put it, 'laugh at a bagpiper', seem to me shrewd observers of the human condition, creatures whose approbation and friendship have to be painstakingly won. Parrots don't curry favour like lap-dogs.

Nowadays, with many psittacine species greatly endangered by environmental hazards and illegal and unscrupulous catching, there is a welcome boom in interest in and concern for parrots worldwide. Their value in financial terms soars, no bad thing for the birds themselves if it makes humans treasure them more, and there are new and fruitful developments in captive reproduction and rearing of an expanding range of species. In my own field of exotic animal medicine, specialist veterinarians with particular interest and skills in psittacine diseases and surgery are contributing more and more to better health for these animals.

But still there exists a great need for more information and assistance to be made available to both the *aficionados* and the devoted pet parrot owners. So often I come across well-meaning and doting parrot fanciers who know virtually nothing about the magnificent creatures that they possess. Birds are still bought from dealers who give little or no, or sometimes erroneous, advice as to their proper maintenance.

Now at last, a comprehensive, clearly laid out guide to things parrot is at hand. Rosemary Low is an internationally acknowledged expert on these creatures and her instructions on everything to do with parrots, together with fascinating information on the wild and gorgeously-coloured world of the family Psittacidae, including the rarest and least-known species, are masterly.

Even the most inexperienced owner of a foul-mouthed African Grey with a penchant for chocolate drops and an aversion to anything in trousers, can now reach for the 'bible' and dip into it with confidence, profit and much pleasure.

DAVID C. TAYLOR BVMS, FRCVS, FZS
KEIGHLEY, YORKSHIRE

Introduction

Parrots are many things to many people. They may be cherished and adored pets (in sensitive care), irreplaceable companions (to the lonely, aged or housebound), perhaps even an unwanted nuisance (in the wrong hands), or an absorbing hobby (to the breeder with a few aviaries). They may be the means of earning a living (to dealers and importers, professional breeders and even trainers) or, to the uninitiated, 'the birds that talk' in the local zoo. To me they are a way of life.

A never ending source of joy and satisfaction, they are also the cause of frequent disappointment and heartbreak, as is inevitable with all livestock. Involved with parrots before I left school, it was not long until they took over my professional life, too, first as deputy editor of the weekly magazine *Cage and Aviary Birds*, then as a freelance writer and author on psittacines, and now as curator of the world's most comprehensive collection of parrots, Loro Parque in Tenerife.

There is so much to learn about these fascinating birds that a lifetime of study can reveal only the tip of the iceberg. I am privileged to work with over 200 species and every day with them throws more light on their behaviour, their needs, their beauty and their personalities.

The beginner has a whole new world of discovery ahead and a thousand and one questions. Many of these can be answered only as the result of personal experience: others, I hope, will be found in the pages which follow. But there will be many unanswered questions because no two parrots are precisely alike: what suits one is not good for another. So observe your birds very carefully and spend much time with them. Only in this way will you develop the rapport which is essential for success.

ROSEMARY LOW
LORO PARQUE, TENERIFE

Features of a parrot

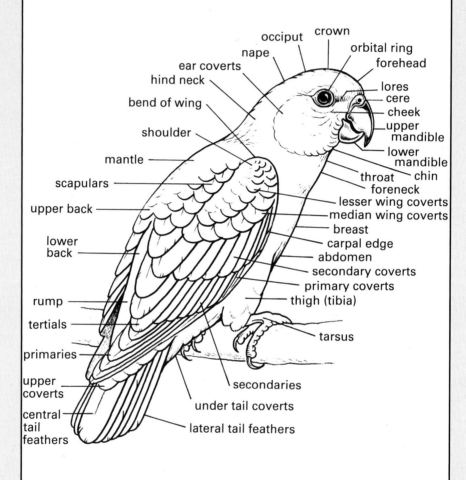

crown
occiput
orbital ring
nape
forehead
ear coverts
hind neck
lores
cere
bend of wing
cheek
shoulder
upper mandible
mantle
lower mandible
scapulars
throat
chin
foreneck
upper back
lesser wing coverts
median wing coverts
breast
lower back
carpal edge
abdomen
secondary coverts
primary coverts
thigh (tibia)
rump
tertials
tarsus
primaries
upper coverts
secondaries
central tail feathers
under tail coverts
lateral tail feathers

ACCIDENT PREVENTION

One of the joys of pet-bird ownership is allowing a bird to share one's room or house, rather than having it confined to a cage. Unfortunately, however, many accidents can befall a bird which has such freedom. Birds are highly inquisitive and, like young children, should not be left unattended.

The risk of accident can be reduced by taking the following precautions before letting a bird out of its cage:

1 Close all doors and windows. Place a screen or guard across an open fireplace.
2 If the windows are not protected by net curtains, close the ordinary curtains on the first two or three occasions on

Before allowing your parrot its freedom within the house, ensure that all potential hazards are removed and doors and windows closed.

which a bird is let out of its cage, to prevent it from flying into the window. If it does so at speed, it could break its neck.
3 Do not allow birds their freedom in the kitchen – a highly hazardous place. They could fall into containers of water or fat, land on a hot stove (remember that an electric hot plate retains heat for a long time after being switched off), or inhale toxic fumes. One of the most frequent accidents, which cannot be warned against too often, results when cookware, coated with Teflon

or some other non-stick material, is heated while empty. The fumes given off if this coating is allowed to burn are lethal to birds. They die in minutes. Fumes from self-cleaning ovens are also dangerous.
4 Birds are more sensitive to fumes than humans (which is why canaries were formerly used to detect gas in coal mines). Therefore do not use aerosols in a room occupied by a bird. Insect sprays are also dangerous. Keep a dog or cat out of doors for a couple of hours after it has been sprayed for fleas. Remove all birds from the house if a room has to be fumigated.
5 Do not allow a bird its freedom in a room where an electric fan is operating.
6 If birds have access to a bathroom, keep the lavatory seat lid down. Cover any other water container, such as an aquarium.
7 Remove or replace lead items, such as lead curtain weights. Do not use lead paint in areas to which birds have access. Lead is highly toxic.
8 Remove pot plants and cacti: some are poisonous.
9 Do not leave matches where birds will have access to them. They, too, are toxic.
10 Certain felt-tipped marker pens are extremely toxic. Pens and pencils should also be removed from reach.
11 A parrot could be killed, or badly shocked, if it bit through the lead to an electrical appliance. Make sure these are not exposed.
12 Cats, dogs and other household pets are a great source of danger to the smaller parrots.

Other household pets can be a source of danger to parrots.

A double Yellow-headed Amazon (*Amazona ochrocephala oratrix*), aged sixteen days.

Agapornis – see *LOVEBIRDS*

Alisterus – see *KING PARRAKEETS*

AMAZON PARROTS (*Amazona*)
Amazons form one of the largest, most distinctive and well-known groups of parrots. There are about twenty-six species (opinions vary as to whether some should be considered as species or sub-species). They originate from South and Central America, and also the Caribbean Islands.

In size they range from about 24 cm (9½ in) in the smallest sub-species of the Spectacled Amazon (*A. albifrons nana*) and the closely related Yellow-lored Amazon (*A. xantholora*) to about 46 cm (18 in) in the magnificent and greatly endangered Imperial Amazon (*A. imperialis*).

All but one species of Amazon are basically green with contrasting markings on the head and tail (and also on the wings, but this is evident in most species only when they are in flight). Recognition can be made mainly by head coloration which varies from unremarkable to extremely beautiful. Pronounced sexual dimorphism is confined to one species, *xantholora*. The body shape does vary but most Amazons are compact and solid in appearance and the beak and feet are strong. The tail is fairly short and square.

Personality varies greatly from species to species and also among individuals. Some, such as the Yellow-fronted Amazon (also called Yellow-crowned), the Double Yellow-headed and the Yellow-naped (all sub-species of *ochrocephala*), and the Festive Amazon (*A. festiva*) are wonderful mimics and can copy human speech, and laugh and sing.

Many Amazons have wonderful qualities as pets, but most have the disadvantage of indulging in regular periods of screaming (morning and evening). This fact must be borne in mind because it is serious enough to disturb other occupants of the house, as well as neighbours. At their best, however, Amazons are affectionate, playful and amusing.

Many pet birds are devoted to one person, or will tolerate attention from men or from women but not both. My own pet of twenty-five years is a Yellow-fronted Amazon – a female who dispels the myth that parrots prefer humans of the opposite sex to themselves. She does not tolerate men (or other Amazons!). Amazons can bite hard, if excited or teased, and are not recommended as children's pets.

As aviary birds Amazons are extremely rewarding subjects, providing they are tame. Most wild-caught adults will also become less nervous in time. Fortunately, with every year that passes, the proportion of aviary-bred to wild-caught birds increases.

Individual preferences in diet are very noticeable in this group, and thus a very wide variety of items should be offered. The basic diet can consist of a mixture of soaked or sprouted sunflower and/or safflower seed, boiled maize, sprouted mung beans and boiled peanut kernels in one container. Another container can be used for dry seeds: approximately equal parts of sunflower or safflower, canary, oats, buckwheat, pine nuts and a little hemp in winter. Many Amazons also relish a millet spray. A third container should be provided for fruits and vegetables.

A very wide variety of table scrap items are enjoyed by Amazons: cooked vegetables, lean meat, bread, toast, cake, pasta, rice, yoghurt, cheese and the occasional crisp as a treat. In moderation these are excellent. Pet Amazons greatly look forward to meal times!

Just prior to the breeding season, and until the end of this period, bread and milk, or a wholewheat bread mixture can be given. The latter is used by many successful breeders in the USA. To the wholewheat bread mixture is added a little raw egg, grated carrot and endive, for example. This is then baked.

Amazons are not the easiest parrots to induce to breed in captivity. Many pairs are infertile, or make no attempt to nest: the latter should be moved to a new location or given new partners. Infertility often stems from the fact that the male and female have not come into breeding condition at the same time.

Amazons usually lay only one clutch per year, although some females can be induced to lay a second clutch if the eggs are removed for artificial incubation. Generally speaking, the smaller and medium-sized Amazons, such as the Cuban (*A. leucocephala leucocephala*), Blue-fronted (*A. aestiva aestiva*) and Yellow-fronted (*A. ochrocephala*), are easier to breed than the large species.

Sex can be determined surgically or by feather follicle sexing. It is impossible to sex them by sight and even those very familiar with Amazon behaviour may guess wrongly.

Amazons lay two to four eggs (only rarely one or five) which are incubated for twenty-five to twenty-eight days by the female. In most countries, April or May is the usual time of egg-laying by captive birds, but eggs are occasionally laid as early as February or March. The young spend eight or nine weeks in the nest. Immature plumage is generally, although not always, duller than that of the adults.

A certain indication of immaturity is the eye colour. In the majority of adult Amazons, the iris of the eye is orange (in a few species, e.g. the rare Jamaican Black-billed Amazon (*A. agilis*) it is dark brown). In all young birds, however, it is greyish-brown, changing to dull orange (where applicable) by the age of about five months. An Amazon required as a pet should be obtained before the eye colour changes. This is the only guarantee that the bird is very young.

Amazons do very well in suspended aviaries in a suitable climate. The minimum recommended length is 2.7 m (9 ft). Traditional-type aviaries are also suitable.

Anodorhynchus **MACAWS** – see under *HYACINTHINE MACAW*

ANTIBIOTICS
Antibiotics are an important facet of veterinary medicine. They should be used only as prescribed by a veterinarian and never as a precautionary measure. Birds

Fresh greenfoods such as sowthistle are an important part of the diet of most Amazons. Seen here are two Mealy Amazons (*Amazona farinosa farinosa*).

which receive antibiotics on a regular basis will become resistant to them.

The same is true of anti-fungal preparations. In the USA, for example, some breeders give hand-reared chicks Nystatin (a fungicide) to prevent them getting candidiasis. By doing this, however, they disturb the balance of the intestinal flora.

A competent veterinarian will obtain a faecal sample from the bird to be treated. From this he or she will prepare an antibiogram, that is, the faecal sample will be cultured on a plate, using several different types of antibiotics. In this way it will be discovered which antibiotic should be the most effective. Valuable time can be wasted when a broad-spectrum antibiotic is given, hoping that it will cure the problem.

After a few days it may be necessary to change to a different antibiotic if the first has not proved effective. With sick birds time is a precious element: all too often a bird's life is lost because the wrong treatment has been prescribed.

A veterinarian needs to know the approximate weight of a bird that is to be given antibiotics, to ensure that the correct dosage is used.

Aprosmictus **PARRAKEETS** – see *CRIMSON-WINGED PARRAKEETS*

 Ara **MACAWS** – see *MACAWS (Ara)*

Aratinga **CONURES**
These Conures originate from Mexico, Central America and from all the tropical regions of South America. The size range of the species is between 23 cm (9 in) and 36 cm (14 in).

This is not an easy group for the uninitiated to recognise, as there is great variation in size, and, although most members of the genus are mainly green, there are some dramatic exceptions. The long tapered tail is common to all members of the genus, however.

This genus could be divided into three groups:
1 The minority – Sun, Jendaya and Queen of Bavaria's (Golden) Conures, which are brilliantly coloured. The latter is uncharacteristically large, with a very large beak. Its coloration is unforgettable, being all golden yellow. An exceptionally intelligent and interesting bird, its drawbacks are its high price and its very loud, harsh voice.
2 Another group is basically green, with red markings on the head and/or scattered red feathers in the region of the head and neck. Given the similarity of some species in immature plumage to other species, identification of this group can be difficult. For example, the Mitred (*A. mitrata*) and Red-masked (*A. erythrogenys*) Conures are easily distinguished in adult plumage and also in the first immature plumage.

On leaving the nest, Mitred Conures are duller red on the head than adults and also have less red, whereas young Red-masked have only a narrow band of brownish-red on the forehead. At about six months old, however, both species have similar scattered red feathers on the head. They can best be distinguished by the larger size of *mitrata* and by the colour of the skin surrounding the eye, which is yellowish in *erythrogenys* (deeper yellow in adults) and white in *mitrata*.
3 The remaining members of the genus are mainly green with dull or contrasting colours on the head, such as orange or blue.

Behaviourally, they are all very much alike, except perhaps that of the Queen of Bavaria's Conure, which seems different but is really only exaggerated. They will all threaten a possible enemy by swaying, ruffling the feathers of the head and shrieking loudly. All have unpleasant voices, thereby disqualifying themselves from many aviaries.

The diet should consist of a mixture of small seeds, such as canary, white millet, oats or groats, buckwheat, a little hemp and small sunflower seeds. They can also be offered a mixture of soaked or sprouted sunflower seeds, sprouted mung beans, boiled peanut kernels, chopped apple, orange, carrot and spinach. Most fruits, such as grapes and pear, will be relished, also spray millet.

Many species of *Aratinga*, especially those in the first and second groups, breed very readily in captivity. They are excellent parents and will also foster the young of other species. They generally lay three or four eggs, which are incubated by the female for about twenty-five days.

Chicks are fairly well covered in white down (yellow in Sun Conures) on hatching. They have a loud food-soliciting cry which is something like that of Amazon parrots. The young spend about eight weeks in the nest, venturing out for short periods only at first, and always returning to the nest to sleep.

The Sun Conure is considered the most beautiful of the smaller members of the genus and is perhaps the most sought-after. The vivid yellow and orange of its plumage ensures that there is always a demand for the young, thus the price is quite high, although not out of reach for most breeders, unlike that of the Queen of Bavaria's Conure.

Many species of *Aratinga* will breed in suspended aviaries, traditional aviaries or large cages. Plumage is alike in male and female, and thus surgical or chromosome sexing is recommended. They usually commence to breed at two years old. Some species are single-brooded, others are double-brooded. Hardy and easy to feed, they can be recommended for beginners.

AVIARY

This term is applied to a large cage used for keeping birds, generally out of doors and with a solid floor.

The most usual design is one with a framework of timber (metal for very destructive species), the sides and roof of welded mesh (often called hardware cloth in the USA) and a sheltered or totally enclosed area for roosting.

The following aspects should be taken into consideration before building an aviary:
1 Planning permission – is this required from any local authority?
2 The site – this should be in a sheltered position and preferably in view of the house, but, for security reasons, not too evident to passersby. (Thefts of parrots are common and a constant source of worry to keepers of these attractive birds.) The aviary should not be in a position where it will disturb or annoy neighbours. It should be on flat land not liable to flooding. Allow for expansion: more aviaries are likely to follow and servicing them is easier in a compact area.
3 The type of structure – there are many possible designs and layouts. If you can, visit a few parrot breeders before starting to build, to ask for ideas and advice. Ask them how their ideal set-up would differ from that currently in use, and thus profit from their mistakes! Altering aviaries is expensive, usually impracticable and often impossible.
4 The setting – a single aviary or range of aviaries can be incorporated into a garden in a most attractive manner. It can be set amid trees, surrounded by

Planting with shrubs and vines can enhance the appearance of garden aviaries.

A neatly built structure, such as this range of aviaries for macaws, will be the focal point of any garden.

flowers and covered in non-poisonous flowering vines, such as honeysuckle, Russian vine or passion flower. It then becomes the focal centre of the garden.

5 Before beginning to build, carefully consider the importance of making the aviary floor vermin-proof. Rats, mice and other rodents are a health hazard and a threat to the lives of aviary occupants: they also consume enormous amounts of food. No matter how well an aviary of conventional design is constructed, or how small the wire mesh, the enclosure will not be vermin-proof unless the floor is made of concrete, or 9-mm (³/₈-in) welded mesh is buried under the ground. Concrete is a hygienic material, provided that regular hosing or scrubbing is carried out. A concrete floor should be constructed so that it slopes slightly towards a drainage channel.

Alternatively (and I prefer this for lories), shingle (large stones) makes an excellent base, regular hosing being all that is required to keep it clean.

It should be noted that soil floors are highly unsatisfactory. They are impossible to clean thoroughly and can only be sterilised with a blow lamp. They are not recommended.

6 The construction – tubular steel is recommended for the framework. Initially it is a little more expensive than wood, but, following construction, there is no maintenance. Unlike wood, it will last a lifetime. It cannot be destroyed, or its appearance spoilt by the occupants. Various shaped joints can be purchased and joined together using a plumber's pipe wrench. Wire can be pop-rivetted to it, using a thin strip of metal.

7 The shelter – this can be open-fronted or totally enclosed, according to the climate and location. In Britain, northern Europe and the northern states of the USA, a fully enclosed shelter is recommended. The birds can be kept inside in inclement weather and lighting and heating can be employed if necessary. (See *INFRA-RED LAMP.*) The shelter must be light, with a window in the side or roof, or birds will refuse to enter.

Covering a glass window with welded mesh is essential to prevent escapes in the event of breakage. Alternatively, glass with inlaid welded mesh can be used if the price is not prohibitive. Locate the entrance to the shelter so that roosting birds are not in a draught. Cover the roof with roofing felt to ensure that it is waterproof. To create an attractive appearance on a sloping roof, roofing tiles can be used.

The roof of the flight must be covered for part of its length, preferably over the highest perch – the preferred roosting location of birds which do not sleep in their nest-boxes. The entire roof can be made of welded mesh, the additional cover being placed above this.

8 The door – situate this where there is least risk of escape. In a single aviary, a safety porch

(double doors, one being closed before the next is opened) is advisable. In a range of aviaries, a service passage situated along the back of the shelters is strongly recommended. The roof of the passage can be covered.

If the door into the aviary opens into the service passage, there is no possibility of escape. Every aviary must have its own access door. Entrance via another aviary not only causes disturbance, but is a hazard: should a door be left open, another bird may enter, with fatal results. Many parrots will instantly kill any other bird which enters their territory.

9 The feeding hatch – this eliminates the need to enter the aviary at feeding time, thus reducing disturbance to the occupants (this is especially important when they are breeding). It also reduces the risk of birds escaping and is essential in aviaries lacking a safety porch. The hatch should be just large enough to admit the food and water containers. These can be hooked onto the welded mesh near the hatch, or placed on a shelf below it. The hatch should be hinged at the top, so that if it is left unfastened, it automatically drops down. Alternatively, it can be constructed on a revolving principle, i.e. the actual shelf rotates, to reveal the containers which are slotted into the shelf or clipped into special holders. In this case, a wire guard on one end of the shelf, or a strip of welded mesh surrounding it, and at the same height as the hatch, will prevent escapes.

B

Barnardius PARRAKEETS

These large parrakeets, which range in size from 33–38 cm (13–15 in), including the long tail, are mainly green, with contrasting areas of blue and yellow, and also red or black in some sub-species. They originate in Australia.

These birds are unsuitable as pets, in both behaviour and temperament. They are at their best in a long aviary, because they need a lot of exercise. Suspended cages are not recommended, because their tails soon become damaged in this type of accommodation. They do best in enclosures which are at least 4.5 m (15 ft) long and 2.1 m (7 ft) high.

Among the more highly priced, and usually less free-breeding Australian parrakeets, these parrakeets are not considered suitable for beginners.

A most attractive feature of these birds is the way they waggle their broad tails from side to side when excited, even in flight. Their plumage, of various shades of green and yellow, generally lacks sharply contrasting colours, except for the Port Lincoln Parrakeet, which has a black head.

Sexual dimorphism is either not very marked or does not exist.

There are two species. Barnard's Parrakeet (*B. barnardi barnardi*) is dark green with a dark red frontal band, light blue on the cheeks, shoulders and wing margins, dark blue on the mantle and the tip of the tail, with a yellow nuchal collar and yellow on the lower breast. Females are usually duller. Young birds have a brownish crown and nape and a greyish-green back and mantle.

A most attractive sub-species is the softly marked Cloncurry Parrakeet (*B. b. macgillivrayi*). Mainly pale green, it has part of the cheeks blue and the nuchal collar and abdomen yellow. Young birds have a dull red frontal band.

The Port Lincoln (*B. zonarius zonarius*) is a very handsome bird. It has part of its cheeks blue but the head is otherwise black, or more brownish-black in some

A feeding hatch is recommended – to save time and prevent disturbing the aviary occupants.

females. The abdomen and also the nuchal collar are yellow. Plumage is otherwise mainly dark green.

The Twenty-eight Parrakeet (*B. z. semitorquatus*) receives its unusual name from its call, which is said to resemble this number. Its plumage differs from that of the Port Lincoln in that the abdomen is green, not yellow.

These birds should be offered as much greenfood as possible, both before the breeding season, to stimulate them to nest, and during the rearing period. They extract the juices from the stems as well as eating the leaves. Carrot, apple, corn on the cob and other fruits and vegetables should be offered as well as a good variety of seeds, such as canary, oats or groats, hemp, buckwheat, white millet, sunflower and safflower. They are very fond of hawthorn berries.

Members of this genus lay four to six eggs, and occasionally as many as seven. These are incubated by the female for nineteen days. These birds are generally single-brooded, but can prove prolific in a more favourable climate than that of Britain, for example.

BEAK
This is one of the distinctive features by which members of the parrot family are recognised.

In parrots, the upper and lower mandible is hinged to the skull, giving vertical movement. The upper surface of the beak is renewed, a little at a time, in an irregular shedding process. The beak actually consists of layers of cells, renewed by proliferation from the basal layer as the outer layers die and become keratinized. Above the upper mandible is a soft, thickened area, known as the cere. In some parrots, such as Eclectus, this is feathered.

In some species there is sexual dimorphism of the beak colour and shape. In *Psittacula* parrakeets, Eclectus Parrots and one sub-species of a *Bolborhynchus* parrakeet, males and females have different bill coloration. In Keas, the beak is longer and more curved in the male.

Chicks within the egg develop an egg tooth, near the tip of the upper mandible, with which to pierce the shell when they hatch. The myth that this is shed after a few days is

perpetuated in almost every book on birds! In fact, as the chick and its bill grow, the egg tooth forms part of the beak. It can still be observed in some chicks as old as three weeks.

There are a variety of different beak shapes in different species, the shape being adapted to feeding habits. One of the best adapted is that of the Red-capped Parrot (*Purpureicephalus spurius*), known as the Pileated Parrakeet outside Australia. It feeds mainly on seeds, especially those of the marri (*Eucalyptus calophylla*). The narrow, elongated upper mandible, and the gap between the two mandibles, appear to be an adaptation for feeding on the seeds of the marri, which are enclosed in a bowl-shaped pod with a rim. The bowl is impenetrable; the seeds can be reached only through the top of the pod.

The parrot with the narrowest, most elongated bill is the Slender-billed Conure (*Enicognathus leptorhynchus*) from Chile. (Its beak shape is not unlike that of the Slender-billed Cockatoo, which is a ground-feeding bird.) This conure is equally adept at extracting pips from apples or at digging in the ground – yet the reason for its unusual bill shape is not known.

The size of the beak is also related to feeding habits. The largest beak of any parrot (also the largest in relation to body size) is that of the Hyacinthine Macaw

A year after breaking off nearly half of its upper mandible in an accident, the beak of this Maximilian's Parrot (*Pionus maximiliani maximiliani*) had grown back almost to the normal length.

(*Anodorhynchus hyacinthinus*); its enormous strength enables it to open any nut. Brazil nuts are opened as easily as a Grey Parrot would extract a peanut from its shell.

Many captive parrots suffer accidents to the beak, usually to the upper mandible, which may be ripped or broken off in its entirety. If this is the case, it will never grow again and, except for a lory (which can survive on a liquid diet), there is little chance that the bird will survive. However, if even a small part of the mandible remains, it will grow again. This will take months, possibly over a year in severe cases, but provided that the bird survives the initial shock, it will live and can learn to eat soft items of food.

In some parrots, growth of the beak may be abnormally rapid, or perhaps irregular as the result of an injury. In such cases regular trimming is necessary. This is best carried out by a veterinarian who has the proper tools, such as an electric drill or file. A sharp pair of nail clippers can be used for small birds. Overgrowth of the beak may simply be due to lack of wood (preferably fresh branches) for gnawing. Some species, such as Fig Parrots, will quickly acquire overgrown beaks if wood is not provided.

BITING

There are three basic reasons why a parrot bites: out of fear, excitement or sheer high spirits, and out of maliciousness. The latter is impossible to cure. Birds which bite for no reason other than because they enjoy doing so, are best used for breeding rather than being kept as pets. Most parrots, even tame ones, will bite out of fear – when caught, for example, and held in the hand. Many parrots, which are tame enough to climb all over their owners, will bite if hands are closed around their bodies, or if certain parts of their bodies are touched.

Some hand-reared parrots, macaws and Greys, for example, go through a stage, at about six months old, when they become very boisterous and excitable and start to nip. From the outset, they should be tapped lightly on the beak and the command 'No!' given. They can thus be made to

understand that such behaviour is not acceptable.

Tame birds may also bite out of jealousy, for example when another parrot is placed too close to the bird while it is on its owner. The tame one cannot bite the intruder, so it bites its owner instead. A tame bird may also bite out of frustration or temper, for example on being returned to its cage when it does not wish to go.

BLACK COCKATOOS

The Black Cockatoos are very large parrots, totally distinct from other cockatoos because their plumage is almost entirely black. There are two genera: *Calyptorhynchus* (three species) and *Probisciger* (one species).

Calyptorhynchus originates from Australia. These are extremely beautiful and highly intelligent birds. Sexual dimorphism is obvious or only slight. They range in size from 50–65 cm (20–26 in). They are rare in captivity.

The diet in captivity should be mainly seeds and nuts, such as sunflower, canary seeds, peanuts, pine nuts, walnuts, Brazil nuts, and, in Australia, the seeds of casuarina, eucalyptus, Banksia and acacia. The White-tailed Black Cockatoo needs more greenfood than the other species.

Although rare in captivity, the Banksian or Red-tailed Black Cockatoo (*C. magnificus*) is the best-known member of the genus. The male is all black, except for a broad band of scarlet on the tail feathers. The tail is barred with red and black in the female, whose head and shoulders are marked with yellow spots.

Its length is 60 cm (23 in). Most immature birds resemble the female, but some young males leave the nest in adult plumage. This is normally acquired at two years and nine months.

This cockatoo occurs in eastern, northern and south-western Australia, being more common in the north. It usually nests in eucalyptus trees. One egg is laid, but occasionally two. Incubation is carried out by the female for twenty-eight days. The young spend twelve to thirteen weeks in the nest. In the wild they stay with their parents until they nest again during the following year.

The nature of this species is

Amazons

Vinaceous Amazon *(Amazona vinacea)* – another Brazilian species threatened by loss of habitat.

Above: Finsch's Amazon *(Amazona finschi)* used to be freely available, but the export of Mexican parrots is no longer permitted.

Pretre's Amazon *(Amazona pretrei)* – a rare species from Brazil.

Lilacine Amazon *(Amazona autumnalis lilacina)* from Ecuador – rare in captivity and declining in the wild.

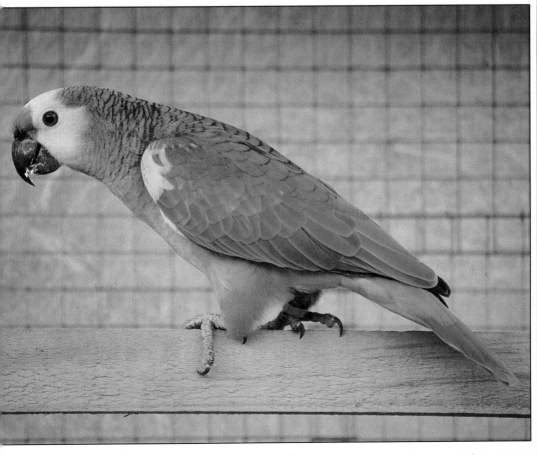

Blue-fronted Amazons *(Amazona aestiva xanthopteryx)*, which are imported today, originate from Paraguay and Argentina.

exceptionally gentle and affectionate. They seldom use their large beaks in defence.

Hand-reared birds, especially males, crave human attention. This can be a problem, in that they can become imprinted on people and are then useless for breeding purposes. They should be introduced to their own species as soon as they are independent. They are nervous and sensitive at this stage, and the introduction must be made with extreme care.

The glossy Black Cockatoo (*C. lathami*) is distinguished from the Banksian Cockatoo by its brownish head coloration and smaller size. Some birds have irregular orange-yellow markings on the head and neck. The female has the red tail band, barred with black and speckled with yellow: there are no yellow spots on the body.

In length it is about 50 cm (19–20 in). Immature birds cannot be sexed: they are all spotted and barred, but by one and a half years some males have lost these markings on ear and wing coverts.

This species is found in eastern Australia (central Queensland to eastern Victoria). It feeds almost entirely on the seeds of the casuarina tree. Its nest is a hollow branch in a tree. Only the female incubates the single egg – for about thirty-two days.

Until fairly recently it was believed that maintaining this species in captivity was dependent upon a supply of casuarina seeds, but this is not so. Australian breeders feed these birds mainly on sunflower seed, of which they should have an unlimited supply. The Glossy Cockatoo has never been kept in captivity outside Australia. Like the Banksian, its personality is friendly and affectionate.

There are two sub-species of Black Cockatoo (*C. funereus*): the Funereal or Yellow-tailed (*C. f. funereus*) and the White-tailed or Baudin's Cockatoo (*C. f. baudinii*). The Funereal is brownish-black, the feathers being margined with yellow. The undersides of the tail feathers are yellow, freckled with brownish-black (more prominently in the female). Her ear coverts are also a brighter yellow. In the White-tailed, the male's ear coverts are greyish, otherwise the areas of plumage which are yellow on the

Funereal, are white. In both sub-species, the bill is dark grey in the male and horn-coloured in the female.

A woodland bird, found in small groups, the Funereal occurs in eastern and south-eastern Australia, and also Tasmania, and the White-tailed in the south-western corner of Western Australia. Sadly, it is endangered by habitat destruction. Breeding information is similar to that given for the Banksian Cockatoo.

There are few *C. funereus* in captivity, especially outside Australia. Their personality is aloof – totally different to that of the other two members of the genus.

The Palm Cockatoo (*Probosciger aterrimus*) originates from New Guinea and Cape York Peninsula in northern Australia. The female is usually smaller than the male, with a shorter upper mandible, but the size of this bird varies between about 70 and 80 cm (28–32 in) according to locality of origin. It is rare in captivity.

A White-tailed Black Cockatoo (*Calyptorhynchus funereus baudinii*).

It has an entirely grey-black plumage, very long, narrow crest feathers, and a large area of bare red facial skin (pale pink in birds in poor condition). The tongue is unusual, being red tipped with black. In immature birds, the feathers of the underparts and the under wing coverts are margined with pale yellow. On leaving the nest, young birds' beaks are edged with white and the skin surrounding their eyes is white.

Its diet in captivity should be similar to *Calyptorhynchus*, plus almonds, for which they have a great liking. Some Palm Cockatoos will eat fruit, such as banana, apple and pear.

Captive breeding has been achieved in a few collections in Europe and Australia.

This species builds a platform of twigs inside its nest (to protect eggs or young from excessive rainfall). The single egg is incubated by both male and female, or by the female only, for about thirty-four days. The young bird spends about twelve weeks in the nest.

This is another gentle species. Wild-caught birds tend to be very shy. The trade in this species is not likely to continue, and thus captive breeding is of the greatest importance.

BLINDNESS

Blindness in parrots can result from injury, infection, poisoning and, especially in aged birds, cataracts. When affected by the latter, there may be partial vision. A bird which is blind may have an eye missing, or one eye which looks glazed or opaque. Sometimes only its behaviour indicates that it is blind, but one can easily test for vision by moving one's hand towards the suspected blind eye.

When a bird becomes totally blind, the decision may have to be made whether or not to end its life. This must depend entirely on individual circumstances. Some birds may be hardly inconvienced at all by blindness, incredible as this may seem. At Loro Parque there is a totally blind female Yellow-bibbed Lory (*Lorius chlorocercus*), a species from the Solomon Islands, which is very rare in captivity. She is an extremely valuable breeding bird. To watch her moving about the aviary it is hard to believe that she is blind until she descends to the ground and begins to use her beak to feel for the sides of the aviary.

The quality of this bird's life is hardly impaired by her blindness, but in other cases, such as where this condition is associated with senile debility, it would be kinder to have a blind bird put to sleep. There is, however, no cause to end the life of a tame pet bird which has become blind if it can still enjoy its food and the attentions of its owner and, indeed, still be a source of pleasure to the household.

BLUE-RUMPED PARROT – see *Psittinus*

Bolborhynchus **PARRAKEETS**
These parrakeets originate in Central America and the western part of South America.

The smallest of the neotropical parrakeets, the diminutiveness of these birds lends them a special charm. Although their plumage is quite different, members of the public often mistake them for budgerigars because most species of *Bolborhynchus* are similar to these little birds in size and shape. The tail varies, however, from long and tapered to short.

Only the Lineolated is well established in captivity – and only a few in European countries. Most newly imported birds are difficult to establish, those from high altitudes (especially the Aymara) being extremely difficult. The death rate is so high that the capture and export of wild-caught birds should be discouraged. Caring aviculturists should buy only captive-bred birds, and there are few of these. Unless more breeders concentrate on these totally delightful little birds, they will be lost to aviculture. This would be regrettable, because their quiet voices and small size make them ideal for apartment-dwellers.

The diet for *Bolborhynchus* should consist of a mixture of small seeds (such as canary, millet, groats, hemp and small sunflower seeds), spray millet, seeding grasses, chickweed, dandelion, spinach, carrot, apple, orange and, when chicks hatch, bread and milk, or a proprietary rearing food.

They will breed in small cages, and a nest-box should be permanently available for roosting.

TOP: The White-eyed Conure *(Aratinga leucophthalmus)* is found over most of tropical South America. BOTTOM: An Hispaniolan Conure *(Aratinga chloroptera)* from Santo Domingo and Haiti.

Conures (1)

The Lesser Patagonian Conure *(Cyanoliseus patagonus patagonus)* is the only sub-species which is common in captivity.

The Blue-throated Conure *(Pyrrhura cruentata)* from Brazil.

A Mountain Parrakeet (*Bolborhynchus aurifrons margaritae*) aged thirteen days.

The Aymara Parrakeet has a large clutch of seven to ten eggs: other members of the genus have a smaller clutch, usually three to five. The incubation period is twenty-three to twenty-four days.

Newly hatched chicks are sparingly covered in down, usually white (but recorded as yellowish in one Aymara chick, although others in the same nest had white down). The chicks' eyes open at about twelve days. The young leave the nest after five to six weeks, or up to eight weeks in the Aymara.

Aymara and Lineolated Parrakeets have proved very prolific. A pair of the latter, belonging to a British breeder, reared thirty-four young between November 1972 and May 1975 – in a cage.

These little parrakeets are very gregarious and breed best within earshot of others of their own genus – or even on the colony system. One London breeder had a successful colony, consisting of three pairs of Lineolated Parrakeets, in an outdoor aviary measuring 2.7 m × 76 cm × 1.8 m high (9 ft × 30 in × 6 ft). On one occasion two females shared the same nest-box.

The Golden-fronted or Mountain Parrakeet (*B. aurifrons*), from Peru, Chile, Argentina and Bolivia, has proved especially difficult to keep alive in captivity. Most imported birds die within the first weeks or months, gradually losing weight, no matter how well they eat. British veterinarian George Smith found, at *post mortem*, that such birds had suffered from osteomalacia (thinning of the bones). He suggested that they require much higher intensities of sunlight than lowland species, in order to manufacture calciferol. (Andean sunlight is indeed intense.) Early deaths could perhaps be prevented if the diet was supplemented with Vitamin D3.

The two species most likely to be encountered are the Aymara or Sierra Parrakeet (*B. aymara*) from Bolivia and Argentina, and the Lineolated (*B. lineola*) from southern Mexico, through Central America to Venezuela, Ecuador and Peru. The Andean Parrakeet (*B. orbygnesius*) differs from the Lineolated in lacking the barred markings. It originates from Peru. Finally, there is the Rufous-fronted (*B. ferrugineifrons*) which is unknown in aviculture. It comes from Colombia.

All are quietly coloured in shades of green and grey and/or yellow. The Sierra or Aymara has dark grey crown and ear coverts (darker and more extensive in the male) and the sides of the neck and throat are whitish-grey. The male's breast is more silvery-grey – most noticeable in young birds on fledging. The plumage is otherwise mainly green, including the long tail. The Golden-fronted has a slightly shorter tail.

Sexual dimorphism is well marked in the nominate race only. The male has a yellow forehead, lores, cheeks, throat, and also part of the breast. In the female, only the cheeks, throat and the sides of the breast are tinged with yellow. This is very confusing, because in other sub-species the male has similar plumage to that of the female of the nominate race. The colour of the legs and bill differs, however.

The Lineolated is most distinctive, with its barred plumage. Most of the feathers of the upper parts have black margins, and there is a black patch on the shoulder. The tail is short and pointed. Its total length is only about 17 cm (7 in), whereas that of the preceding two species is 18 or 19 cm.

BREEDING

This is the aim of vast numbers of people who keep parrots. They consider it the most rewarding and interesting aspect of birdkeeping. I know of no greater satisfaction than putting together two birds, watching them prepare to nest, then lay their eggs, and then observing the development of the chicks. Each newly hatched chick is a fresh miracle whose progress I follow with keen interest. And if it is a rare species, perhaps one that has seldom been raised in captivity, it provides a sense of achievement that nothing else can equal. Breeding is also important because fewer and fewer birds are caught in the wild and exported. Many species will not be available to aviculturists in a few years' time unless captive stocks are built up now.

Breeding different parrot species, from the small lovebirds to the large macaws and cockatoos, is achieved under a multitude of different conditions – in small cages or large aviaries, outdoors and indoors.

Success depends on many factors, the most important of which are:

1 The birds must feel secure, and not be threatened or stressed by other birds or outside influences.
2 They must be correctly fed and housed in order to maintain them in the condition where their normal desire to breed is stimulated.
3 They must have a compatible partner – and this must be of the opposite sex! (Many 'pairs' ultimately prove to be two males or two females.)
4 They require a suitable nesting site (see *NEST-BOXES*).
5 The birds must be suitable for breeding, not too old, in-bred, or possessing some physical defect, such as a tumour near the vent, and they must not be unduly nervous.

In many species that breed freely in confinement, such as cockatiels, lovebirds and Australian parrakeets, these requirements are easy to fulfil. This is why these species are recommended to the beginner. Starting with 'difficult' species is not only discouraging, but does not enable the owner to gain the vital experience needed to be a successful breeder.

Successful breeding does not depend on extravagant facilities or even on the most expensive foods, but on a sympathetic and observant keeper.

The breeder also needs time to observe the birds: without this he or she will not discover if they are incompatible or have problems copulating (there could be a problem as simple as the perch used for copulation being too narrow or placed in an unsuitable position). It is extremely important that owners get to know their birds, and the birds to know them.

BROODERS

Brooders are used for chicks which are being hand-reared. Except in warm climates, where a heat pad can supply the warmth necessary to maintain the chick's body temperature, brooders are indispensable.

They should be made of a material which is easy to clean, such as melamine. Aquariums can be easily adapted to make excellent brooders. All that is needed is a roof of wood or metal into which are fitted two light bulbs attached to a thermostat, or, if the outside temperature is not likely to fluctuate greatly, to a dimmer (such as is used to dim lights in a room).

In cold climates the sides of the aquarium can be insulated by covering them with polystyrene: ceiling tiles are useful for this purpose. I leave the front uncovered, or, in a brooder specially designed for chicks, have the front made of perspex.

Chicks should be easily observable at all times. They are thus also less nervous than when kept in covered containers. They do like to observe what is going on around them! In addition, if not kept in the dark, they will start to feed at an early age.

Two red 60-W bulbs can be used to heat the brooder. These should

Conures (2)

Austral Conures *(Enicognathus ferruginea minor)* – two of five young reared in one nest at Loro Parque.

Above: Weddell's, or the Dusky-headed Conure *(Aratinga weddellii)* is found in Colombia, Ecuador, Peru, Bolivia and Brazil. It is a free-breeding species suitable for the beginner.

The White-eared Conure *(Pyrrhura leucotis leucotis)* is rare in captivity and endangered in the wild.

The high price of the
Queen of Bavaria's,
or Golden Conure
(*Aratinga guarouba*),
makes it suitable
only for experienced
breeders.

This brooder is heated by two electric light bulbs in the roof, which are connected to a room dimmer.

be fitted into the roof: underfloor heating can be dangerous, as chicks are too near the heat source. Small chicks should be kept in containers within the brooder. Older chicks are allowed their freedom, on a false floor of welded mesh. On no account should they be kept on wood shavings: many parrot chicks have died as a result of ingesting these.

Newspaper, wood shavings or any absorbent material can be placed below the wire-mesh base. Chicks kept on welded mesh are less likely to have foot deformities (such as hind toes pointing forward) than those kept on a soft surface. They can be kept on mesh from the age of a few days.

The brooder should also contain a small spill-proof container of water (to provide some humidity) and a reliable thermometer. The digital type is recommended: it is easy to read and has a probe which can be inserted inside the brooder while the thermometer itself stays outside, thus ensuring it is not fouled by the chicks' droppings.

BUYING
Many, many mistakes are made in the purchase of parrots, and some are serious enough to deter the buyer from ever trying again. The most common mistakes are:
1 Buying an adult bird for a pet. An inexperienced person can easily be misled into believing that he or she is buying a youngster. A little research or advice prior to the purchase, or taking the trouble to seek out a breeder of the required species,

would prevent this. It is not possible to tame most adult parrots, especially those which are wild-caught.
2 Buying an unsuitable species as a pet. Cockatoos and macaws, for example, are *not* suitable for the average household. It may present a glamorous picture to walk around with a macaw on one's shoulder, but the reality is usually less attractive – a destructive, noisy, demanding bird with which the owner is unable to cope. The result: a neurotic feather-plucking macaw, irate neighbours and a demented owner. There are people who have the time, and the essential sympathetic attitude, to keep large parrots in a house, but they are a rare minority. Most macaws and cockatoos will live life to the full only in an aviary and with the opportunity to breed.
3 Buying a sick bird. Unfortunately, many wild-caught parrots are fatally diseased, usually as a result of insanitary conditions in the country of origin prior to being exported. The fact that they have been quarantined by the importer does not guarantee good health. Regrettably, many imported birds suffer from aspergillosis, salmonella, or even, as the result of over-medication, a diseased liver. They can survive in this condition for several months.

It is always worth paying more to buy a captive-bred young bird from a reputable breeder. There may be a wait of several months for the species desired, but, if you choose wisely, your parrot could be your companion for the rest of your life. Impulse buying should be resisted by the inexperienced.

It is most important to look for the following signs of poor health: dull eyes, frequently closed, especially if the bird is sleeping for long periods with fluffed-up plumage and resting on two feet. (Adult birds in good health hold their plumage tightly against their bodies and normally rest on one leg.)

Discharge from the eyes or nostrils, or damp or soiled plumage in this area, are indications of disease. Matted faeces, or soiled feathers surrounding the vent are equally serious. Swollen, irritated eyes are a sign of conjunctivitis, or a more serious ailment, such as pox.

Avoid birds with laboured breathing, accompanied by wheezing sounds or obvious pumping movements of the tail. Examine the mouth to ensure that there are no lesions of candida especially in lories or young birds which have been hand-reared.

Look at the beak. It should not be soft or misshapen. This condition, associated with poor plumage (especially in cockatoos), may indicate that the bird is suffering from *PSITTACINE BEAK AND FEATHER DISEASE* (see entry).

If you intend to buy an adult bird as a pet, which is tame and had a previous home as a pet, be sure to enquire whether the bird prefers men or women. Many will *never* change their preference and will fear and/or attack people of the 'wrong' sex.

Be wary of adult birds offered for sale for breeding purposes. There may not be an honest reason for the sale: the bird may be a killer of females, it may break eggs, be infertile or too old to reproduce. Pairs of rare species offered for sale are also often suspect. Young birds should be purchased for breeding in most instances, because they cannot have already been proved useless in this respect and are likely to be a genuine sale.

There are many magazines or publications of specialist societies (those dealing with only one group of parrots, such as lovebirds or Amazons) which carry numerous advertisements from breeders. It is mainly young birds that will be offered for sale, whereas adults of unknown history will be found in pet shops or stores.

C

CAGES

Birdroom Cages

Cages in a birdroom may be used for breeding, for winter accommodation or for housing young birds. Whatever the purpose, the design will not differ greatly. A principal factor should be ease of cleaning. Suitable materials are melamine and marine plywood which has been stained and varnished; this produces a surface which is easy to wipe clean.

Departing from the traditional type of cage with trays which pull out, a design which I have used in an indoor birdroom can be recommended. The cages measured about 91 cm (3 ft) long, 61 cm (2 ft) deep and 70 cm (28 in) high. Construction was of 19-g, 1.25-cm (½-in) welded mesh on a wooden framework. (The floor can be of a larger size of welded mesh, depending on the feeding habits of the species kept; a larger mesh facilitates cleaning.)

The cages stood on legs 10 cm (4 in) high. They actually housed small lorikeets, so plastic cat litter trays were used underneath to contain the liquid droppings. For other species newspaper is excellent. The entrance door measured 25 cm (10 in) square. (It is important to place this in the centre of the cage so that all corners can be reached for cleaning.) Nest-boxes were attached to the outside of the cage to conserve space within, and for ease of inspection.

Where space is at a premium, cages can be in tiers, reaching from ceiling to floor. This is not an ideal arrangement, but the principal disadvantage of inadequate lighting can easily be overcome. I used a small strip light in each cage, 31 cm (12 in) long, connected at the back of the cages to one cable.

The cages described above are suitable for keeping and breeding lovebirds, *Bolborhynchus* parrakeets and, if the length is increased, other small neotropical parrakeets, such as *Brotogeris* species and others of similar size.

The Greater
Sulphur-crested
Cockatoo *(Cacatua
galerita galerita)* – a
pest in Australia, but
cherished and
expensive elsewhere.

Cockatoos (1)

The Umbrella, or White-crested Cockatoo *(Cacatua alba)* from the islands of the Moluccas.

In the Gang Gang Cockatoo *(Callocephalon fimbriatum)* the male is distinguished by his red head.

It is worth noting that some birds actually reproduce more successfully in indoor cages than in outdoor aviaries. One species notable in this respect is the little Goldie's Lorikeet (*Trichoglossus goldiei*) from New Guinea.

Pet Cages

The four principal factors to bear in mind when choosing a cage for a pet bird, are that it must be spacious enough for the bird to be able to stretch its wings fully and to move about freely; that it is a suitable shape, that it will be easy to clean, and that it is attractive in appearance.

Cages with a plastic base are lighter and easier to keep clean than the traditional type with a tray which slides out. Cages with horizontal bars, which allow the bird to climb more easily, are preferable to those with vertical bars. Plastic perches should be replaced by natural branches (renewed regularly, when the bark has been gnawed off and the surface becomes slippery).

Commercially produced cages for large parrots, such as macaws, are very expensive to purchase. Using a 3.6 × 1.8 m (12 × 6 ft)

panel of 12-g, 7.5 × 2.5 cm (3 × 1 in) welded mesh, a cage 1.05 m high × 91 cm × 61 cm (3½ × 3 × 2 ft) can be made that is suitable for a single macaw up to the size of a Green-winged.

Cut off 61 cm (2 ft) at the top and the side of the panel and bend the remaining sheet into shape to give the sides of the cage. The 61 cm (2 ft) off-cut is used to make the roof, floor and door. The sections can be joined using C-clips for 12-g wire. This cage can be made at a very low cost.

Large mesh such as 7.5 × 2.5 cm (3 × 1 in) is very suitable for indoor use where one does not have to worry about rats, mice and sparrows gaining entry and stealing the food. It is more rigid than smaller-mesh wire and therefore easier to work with. Small wire-mesh 'legs' can be put under the cage so that newspaper can be laid beneath it.

Suspended Cages

These are ideal for outdoor use in warm climates. They are raised about 1.2 m (4 ft) off the ground and are supported by something like 19-mm (¾-in) galvanized tubing. A framework of this can be constructed to take any number of cages. The suggested size for medium or small Amazons, *Pionus*, other neotropical parrots and lories is 2.7 × 1 × 1 m high (9 × 3 × 3 ft).

Cockatoos like to be able to walk about on the ground, and Australian parrakeets and some other long-tailed species tend to damage their tails in suspended cages. For other species, it is a question of discovering what suits a particular pair of birds.

The sections of wire used in construction can be joined by C-clips, or by folding the protruding wire, where the mesh is cut, around the piece of mesh to which it is to be joined. If 16-g, 2.5 × 2.5 cm (1 × 1 in) welded mesh is used, it supports itself without sagging. Longer cages than the size suggested will need to be strengthened, using angled metal.

To provide protection from wind, rain and sun, part of the sides and roof can be covered in opaque perspex which is pop-rivetted onto the framework. There must be a door at each end to facilitate catching, which can be

A cage for a pet bird, such as this cockatiel, must be spacious enough for the bird to extend its wings fully and to move around freely. Note that here the plastic perches have been replaced by natural perches which are much better for the bird's feet.

difficult in suspended cages. This is the main disadvantage.

These cages are more hygienic than others, in that the faeces fall through the wire base of the cage, as do small items of uneaten food. The floor can be kept clean by hosing and scraping. It is often stated that birds feel more secure in suspended cages because no one can enter their territory, but the main point in favour of suspended cages, from the keeper's point of view, is the reduced time spent in cleaning and maintenance.

CAIQUES (*Pionites*)
Few more distinctive or delightful genera of parrots exist. Caiques are recognised by their white breast, contrasting with green upperparts and orange or yellow thighs. The stance is usually upright and the tails are square. There is no marked sexual dimorphism. They originate from the Amazon basin and the northern part of South America (Guianas, Brazil, Colombia, Peru, Ecuador and northern Bolivia).

Two species are recognised; the only difference being one of pigmentation. The Black-headed (*P. melanocephala*) has the top of the head and the feet and beak black, and the White-bellied (*P. leucogaster*) has the top of the head pale orange and the feet and beak pale pinkish. In length it is 23 cm (9 in).

The sub-species *pallida* differs from the Black-headed mainly in having the thighs yellow, not orange, and *xanthomeria* differs from the White-bellied in having the thighs and flanks yellow instead of green. There is also a caique from north-west Brazil, (*P. l. xanthurus*) which has the entire tail yellow. It is almost unknown in captivity.

Behaviourally, caiques are among the most fascinating of parrots. They display and vocalise loudly at the slightest provocation, in a shrill penetrating voice. The display is similar to that of some conures, but more exaggerated: they lean forward on the perch and sway their bodies in a circular motion, opening and vibrating the wings at great speed so that they appear a blur, and dilate their pupils so that they blaze red-orange.

Caiques have a great need to gnaw and should be provided with fresh green branches every week. Kept in a small group, they are extremely interesting to watch, but once the group is established no newcomer should be added. They act as one, investigating, feeding and playing, in a manner which is a great pleasure to observe. Colony breeding of Black-headed Caiques is not advised because they are usually too aggressive, or one male will become dominant and take over all the females.

A Yellow-thighed Caique (*Pionites leucogaster xanthomeria*), aged twenty-three days.

With the White-bellied Caique, however, it can be extremely successful. At Busch Gardens, Tampa, Florida, the colony on exhibit for many years produced numerous young. All the birds used the same large nest-box for roosting and breeding. At one time four females were raising as many as seven young!

Caiques are being bred with increasing frequency, but still in small numbers. They are seldom imported these days, thus captive breeding is very important. Probably the most successful breeder of the Black-headed Caique, Tom Ireland, also resides in Florida. When his pairs were separated by other neotropical species, the results were poor; whereas, when moved into adjacent cages, production increased dramatically. The cages are very small, approximately 46 × 91 × 91 cm high (1½ × 3 × 3 ft) and suspended about 91 cm (3 ft) off the ground. There are no solid partitions between these all-wire cages. The first female will lay at the end of December and within a couple of weeks most of the other ten or so pairs will also be on eggs.

The diet of these birds does not differ from that of the other parrots in Tom Ireland's collection. It consists of a mixture of various dry seeds, large quantities of fresh corn on the cob, other vegetables and fruits and a mixture of wholemeal bread, grated carrot and endive. Caiques are extremely fond of fruit and need more than almost any other parrot.

They relish cracked walnuts and cubes of cheese, and some will take bread and milk when rearing young.

Three to four eggs are laid, incubated by the female. The incubation period is usually twenty-five days. The young spend about ten weeks in the nest.

Callocephalon fimbriatum – see *GANG GANG COCKATOO*

Chalcopsitta LORIES

The four lories which comprise this genus have totally contrasting basic colours (black, brown, green and red). They are large, with long, broad tails, their total length being approximately 30 cm (12 in). The skin surrounding the lower mandible is naked (this is also the case with the Dusky Lory, *Pseudeos fuscata*).

The diet consists of nectar and fruit. Corn on the cob and sweetcorn will be eaten by most *Chalcopsitta* species, especially those with young. Some will also consume bread and milk, and mealworms. Many newly imported birds are very conservative feeders.

Imported *Chalcopsitta* lories take three or four years to become sexually mature; captive-bred birds mature more quickly. Two eggs are laid and the incubation period is twenty-four days. They may be single- or double-brooded, depending on climate and whether the young are removed for hand-rearing. Once they start to breed they often prove prolific, but many pairs apparently lack the stimulus or correct conditions to induce breeding.

Three species come from New Guinea.

The Black Lory (*C. atra*) is black with a purple sheen and a blue sheen on the rump. The underside of the tail is red and yellow. Immature birds may have a few, or many, red feathers on any part of the head or body. Bare facial skin

is white in young birds and black in adults.

One of the most unusually coloured of all parrots is

Duivenbode's Lory (*C. duivenbodei*). The basic colour is brown with a golden tinge; the narrow, elongated feathers on the neck are yellow, and the thighs and entire under wing coverts are golden yellow. A striking area of feathers, encircling beak and throat, are also golden yellow. A beautiful contrast is provided by the violet-blue lower back, rump and under tail coverts. Immature birds are much duller, with shorter tails and the facial skin white.

The third member of the genus from New Guinea is the Yellow-streaked Lory (*C. scintillata*). The forehead and crown (or forehead only) are red, and also the thighs and under wing coverts. The upperparts are mainly green and the lower back skyblue. The underparts are brownish on the breast and green on the abdomen, the whole being prominently streaked with yellow. Shaft-streaking (the prominent streak in the centre of the feather) reaches maximum development in this species. Immature birds are much duller, with black instead of red on much of the head, or with a more brownish coloration over all. Full bright adult plumage takes several years to acquire. Mature birds are gaudy but very beautiful.

The Cardinal Lory (*C. cardinalis*) from the Solomon Islands is very rare in captivity because few birds are exported

Duivenbode's Lory (*Chalcopsitta duivenbodei*) – a chick aged fifty-two days.

from those islands. It is, however, common in the wild. Entirely red, with brownish-red on the wings and breast, it has tiny silvery feathers on the bend of the wing. The small beak is red in adults, and brownish in immature birds. The skin surrounding the beak is yellow and black. There is no shaft-streaking in this species.

Charmosyna LORIES

The members of this genus can be divided into two groups – those which have the underparts mainly red, and those in which the plumage is basically green. Four of the fourteen species are reasonably well known in aviculture; the others are virtually unknown. These lories are found in New Guinea and various islands of the Moluccas (Indonesia) and the Pacific.

In captivity, these lories are even more reliant on nectar than other lories, but most will also eat some fruit. Only rarely is seed taken: my own *placentis* relish spray millet.

Most are small, and all are slender, finely proportioned birds. The largest is Stella's (*C. papou stellae*) which is slightly larger in body size than a Perfect Lorikeet (*Trichoglossus euteles*). Its unique feature (for a lory) is the great length of the tail. It seems that this increases with age. In a male known to be at least ten years old, the tail is approximately 38 cm (15 in) long – that is nearly twice the length of the body.

After watching a Stella's Lorikeet for a few seconds, I am always convinced that this is the most beautiful bird in the world. It has extreme grace of form, stunning colour, no loud or discordant notes, but only intriguing, distinctive vocalisations, sexual dimorphism and the longest, fluttering tail of any parrot. Few birds are more fascinating to watch. Stella's make darting movements of the body without moving the feet, jump effortlessly over a companion and, in display, perform exaggerated circular swaying movements.

Unfortunately, their extreme beauty has resulted in them being favoured above all other birds, except Birds of Paradise, for tribal decoration by New Guinea tribesmen. Whole skins are used and the females, with daffodil yellow rump and sides, are probably especially sought after. The male is red in these areas. (Young birds can be sexed in nest feather.) Unusually, there is a melanistic phase which is as common as the red. In this phase the red areas are replaced by black. Two melanistic birds paired together can produce melanistic and red young.

Two eggs are laid. The incubation period is twenty-six days and the young spend between seven and eight weeks in the nest.

Almost similar to Stella's in coloration is the Josephine's Lorikeet (*C. josefinae*). It has a red tail, lacks the central elongated feathers and is slightly smaller. The lower back is yellow in the female, and red in the male. This species has a less extravert personality.

Both the foregoing are found in New Guinea, as is the much smaller Fairy Lorikeet (*C. pulchella*). It measures about 18 cm (7 in). Mainly green above and red below, the male has the under tail coverts red and yellow; in the female they are greenish-yellow, as are the sides of the rump. There are yellow streaks on the upper breast (on a background of green in the sub-species *rothschildi*).

The Fairy Lorikeet has not often been imported and has seldom bred in captivity. It cannot tolerate low temperatures, and thus, rather than move pairs indoors during cold weather, it may be advisable to keep them indoors permanently or, better still, in a small, heated, planted house. Here they are seen at their best.

Under the right conditions they should prove prolific; if one nest fails, more eggs will be laid after about three weeks. This is a totally delightful little bird which deserves the attention of specialist breeders prepared to go to some trouble to establish a species in captivity.

The foregoing remarks apply equally to the Pleasing or Red-flanked Lorikeet (*C. placentis*). One specialist Danish breeder found exactly the right conditions for this most attractive little bird – and reared forty in four years. He used a heated, glass-fronted cage in an indoor birdroom.

As in the other members of the genus known in captivity, incubation is shared by male and female. The young spend about fifty-six days in the nest and can be sexed as soon as they feather (males have red flanks). The Red-flanked occurs in New Guinea, Indonesia (Moluccas) and the Solomon Islands (Bougainville).

Note that the respiration rate in the small *Charmosyna* species is noticeably more rapid than in other small parrots.

CHICKS

Parrot chicks are altricial – that is, on hatching they are totally helpless, are fed by the parents, and have their eyes and ears closed. They may be virtually naked but for a few wisps of down (Eclectus, *Psittacula*), have a small amount of down (*Aratinga* conures), or be densely covered (some lories, *Calyptorhynchus* cockatoos).

The variation in development among the genera is great: the period they spend in the nest varies between only four and a half weeks (*Forpus* parrotlets, budgerigars) and four months (large macaws and cockatoos). For example, Amazon (*Amazona*) parrots, which spend about eight to ten weeks in the nest, weigh between 8–10 g on hatching, according to the species. They have only a few wisps of down. The eyes open at about three weeks and the ears a few days later. The plumage is almost complete by about two months. There is little second down, whereas some parrots (lories and Eclectus, for example) are heavily clothed in second down by three to four weeks of age. The down colour varies from white to light grey, dark grey, or even yellow.

CHICKS, FAILURE TO FEED

There are three basic reasons why birds fail to feed their chicks at all, or suddenly cease to feed them. The first is inexperience. A pair of birds which have never hatched young before sometimes starve their first chicks. Subsequently they may prove to be good parents.

The second reason is that the chick has become chilled or is sick. A chick that is too weak to hold up its head to receive food, cannot be fed by the parents.

On occasions, an experienced pair will cease to feed a chick which is apparently quite healthy. If this chick is removed and hand-fed, it is often found that it will not thrive – that there is something fundamentally wrong with it. The parents knew this instinctively! Experienced parents usually have a good reason for deserting a chick.

Thirdly, a pair may cease to feed all their young because of some stressful environmental disturbance. Examples are disturbance by cats or vermin at night, severe weather conditions, or some unusual happening or loud noise within the vicinity of the aviary. Nest inspection should not cause desertion, except just possibly in the case of very nervous birds whose nest has not previously been examined.

CITES

This is the abbreviation for the

Macaw chicks, such as this Blue and Yellow (*Ara ararauna*), are among the most appealing of young birds.

Convention on International Trade in Endangered Species of Wild Fauna and Flora. Sooner or later the reader will find this mentioned in avicultural literature, as it increasingly affects the availability of species. For the purpose of this Convention, which monitors trade, all species of parrots are placed in one of three categories, Appendix I, II or III, according to whether the species is endangered, threatened or not at risk, respectively.

Representatives from countries throughout the world, which are signatories to CITES, meet every year and propose additions to, or removals from, the various appendices. A vote is taken on the evidence offered to decide whether additions or deletions should be made. In most cases, little information is available on population numbers, only that the population is declining and that it must be protected from trade.

Applications to import or export species on Appendix I or II have to be made to the appropriate authority of the exporting country and each case is decided individually. It may take up to three months to obtain the necessary permission to export an endangered species. Those imported without the necessary documentation are confiscated by Customs if recognised.

In the UK the appropriate authority is the Department of the Environment, Tollgate House, Houlton St, Bristol BS2 9DJ.

The name of the department which deals with CITES documentation in other countries can be obtained by writing to the Secretariat of CITES, 6 rue de Maupas, Case Postale 78, CH 1000 Lausanne 9, Switzerland.

At the time of going to press, the following parrot species were listed in Appendix I (endangered):

Amazona arausiaca
  barbadensis
  brasiliensis
  dufresniana rhodocorytha
  guildingii
  imperialis
  leucocephala
  pretrei
  tucumana
  versicolor
  vinacea
  vittata
Anodorhynchus hyacinthinus
  *leari**
Ara ambigua
  glaucogularis
  macao
  maracana
  militaris
  rubrogenys
Aratinga guarouba
Cacatua moluccensis
Cyanopsitta spixii
Cyanoramphus auriceps forbesi
  novaezelandiae
Geopsittacus occidentalis
Neophema chrysogaster
Ognorhynchus icterotis
Opopsitta diophthalma coxeni
Pezoporos wallicus
Pionopsitta pileata
Probosciger aterrimus
Psephotus chrysopterygius
  pulcherrimus (presumed
  extinct)
Psittacula eques
Psittacus erithacus princeps
Pyrrhura cruentata
Rhynchopsitta pachyrhyncha
  terrisi
Strigops habroptilus

All other species of parrots are listed in Appendix II (threatened), with the exception of *Melopsittacus undulatus* (budgerigar), *Nymphicus hollandicus* (cockatiel) and *Psittacula krameri* (Ringneck Parrakeet). Those who obtain birds imported with CITES papers must retain these papers. Without them it may be difficult or impossible to re-export or sell.

(*also *Anodorhynchus glaucus* if extant)

CLUTCH

A clutch is the term for the number of eggs laid in one breeding period. In parrots it varies from one in the Black Cockatoos (sometimes two), two in Eclectus Parrots, most lories and some cockatoos, three or four in Amazons, *Pionus* and macaws, and four, five, or up to eight in most Australian parrakeets.

The usual clutch size of some other parrakeets is larger; the little *Bolborhynchus aymara*, for example, usually lays eight to ten eggs. Perhaps this indicates that, as in those popular UK garden birds, the tits (*Parus*), the normal life-span of the species is short, or possibly that they breed only under optimum conditions which may not occur every year.

The abnormally large clutches recorded in some Australian species, such as cockatiels and parrakeets – up to twelve eggs – may be the result of domestication. In the wild these species breed only when conditions are favourable, i.e. after rain, when there is an ample supply of food on which to rear their young. Captive birds normally have abundant supplies of food.

In most parrots, eggs are laid every second or third day. In some small species the interval may be as short as thirty-six hours, and in some large ones (notably cockatoos) the interval could be four or five days.

The difference in clutch size between closely related species can be explained by their habitats. More food is available per bird in habitats where there are seasonal fluctuations of climate and plant growth (most of the Australian parrakeets originate from such areas) and, therefore, here the inhabitants lay larger clutches than those from rainforest, for example. In the latter type of habitat, there are no well-marked seasons and availability of food does not vary greatly throughout the year. There is no sudden increase in food supply, therefore clutch sizes are smaller.

In some birds, known as indeterminate layers, the clutch size can be influenced. If eggs are removed as laid, a larger number of eggs than normal will be produced. Owners of single pet budgies, for example, often make the mistake of removing any eggs that are laid, instead of allowing the bird to incubate them. The result is that an enormous number of eggs are laid, possibly severely debilitating the female, or even resulting in her death if adequate calcium is not supplied for egg production.

Other species lay a pre-determined number of eggs in one clutch; these are known as determinate layers and their clutch size cannot be influenced by the removal of eggs.

The number of clutches laid per year also varies. At one extreme there are the almost continuous layers, such as lovebirds (*Agapornis*) and Eclectus Parrots, who will lay again within about three weeks of the eggs or young being removed. Others, such as lories, lay several clutches in the course of one year. Some birds are double-brooded or single-brooded, while others – Amazons, for example – normally lay only one clutch if this proves successful in producing young.

See also *EGGS*.

COCKATIEL (*Nymphicus hollandicus*)

The cockatiel is immensely popular with breeders and pet-bird keepers. It is not a parrakeet, as its long tail leads many to believe, but is very closely related to the cockatoos. This is apparent from its breeding behaviour (male and female take turns in incubating the eggs, for example) and in the appearance of the chicks before they are feathered.

There can be no finer bird to introduce beginners to parrot keeping. Simple to feed, hardy, sexable at a glance, easy to breed, low-priced, long-lived, yet ready to breed at a year old – what more could anyone ask in one bird? It has a pleasant warbling 'song' – which, incidentally, can be used as an indication of sex at an early age (young males start to warble at about three months old).

In recent years the development of numerous attractive colour mutations has enormously increased the cockatiel's popularity with bird fanciers and this has led to thousands discovering that the cockatiel is one of the most wonderful pets it is possible to own. Pretty, intelligent, affectionate, easily tamed and a good mimic of words and whistled tunes, no pet bird gives more enjoyment to a family. Its small size makes it easy and safe for a child to handle, yet being twice the body size of a budgerigar, it is a step towards the larger parrots.

Cockatiels originate from Australia where they occur over most of the continent except for coastal areas. There, their diet consists almost entirely of seeds, and thus they have adapted well to captivity. None have been exported from Australia for many years: all those available have been captive-bred for generations.

More than one third of the cockatiel's total length of 31 cm (12 in) consists of the tail. Its weight is in the region of 90 g. The wild-type bird, from which the mutations have been developed, is mainly grey with the head yellow and a prominent patch of orange on the ear coverts (without which it would be not nearly as attractive). This patch is brighter in the male, as is, normally, the yellow crest. The large white patch on the wing is not fully evident until the bird is seen in flight.

In adult birds, another prominent difference in the sexes is the coloration of the underside of the tail: black in males, and barred with yellow and grey in the female. Young birds resemble females, but have much shorter tails and pinkish ceres.

The most popular mutation is the lutino (often called white, or even albino, but neither of these names is technically correct). It is mainly white or pale yellow (deeper yellow in strains in which breeders have concentrated on colour) with the orange and yellow facial markings retained. This mutation is difficult to sex. Males have a few irregular yellow marks on the underside of wings and tail. In adult females, and in immature birds of both sexes, these areas are faintly, but regularly, barred with yellow.

Several other mutations and countless combinations of mutations (such as cinnamon pearl pied) are being bred. (The breeder who is especially interested in colour mutations is advised to obtain a book on breeding cockatiels.) These include the pied (specialist breeders aim for a bird which is mainly pale yellow with grey on the wings), cinnamon and cinnamon pied (the grey markings are replaced by soft fawn), silver (very light grey) and pearl.

The dietary requirements of cockatiels are easily satisfied. They need a seed mixture, which consists of canary seed, millet and oats or groats and a little sunflower, with the addition of a little hemp and niger during cold weather. Alternatively, budgerigar mixture can be offered in one container and a little sunflower seed in another. Spray millet is relished at all times. Every day a little greenfood should be offered: chickweed, seeding grasses, kale, spinach and other greens, such as the leafy part of celery. Some cockatiels will eat a little apple and carrot; others ignore these foods.

Breeding birds need a nutritious rearing food, such as wholemeal bread and milk, or a drier mixture made from bread, hard-boiled egg and grated carrot, for example. Some will eat the proprietary eggfoods made for canaries.

COCKATOOS (*Cacatua* and *Eolophus*)

Any layman can recognise a cockatoo – a white, crested parrot – but not all cockatoos are white. Several species are black (see *BLACK COCKATOOS*). Two species from Australia have a lot of pink in their body plumage.

One of these, the Roseate, Rose-breasted or Galah (*Eolophus* or *Cacatua roseicapillus*), is generally considered distinct enough in behaviour and appearance to warrant a separate genus. It is grey above and pink below.

Leadbeater's or Major Mitchell's

Cockatoo chicks grow slowly: at 47 days this Umbrella Cockatoo was only half feathered. It weighed 452 g (1 lb).

Cockatoo (*C. leadbeateri*) is also pink below but easily recognised by the spectacular bands of orange in its crest. This is often considered to be the most beautiful of the white cockatoos.

Identification of the other species can be difficult (see the table).

Although many cockatoos are kept as pets, their reign indoors is seldom long. Their loud voices and ability to destroy anything in sight result in most ending up in an aviary.

They *must* have constant occupation for their beaks; part of a fresh cut branch should be given to a caged cockatoo every day, and also something hard, like a leather dog chewy, or a strong chain. If normal food and water containers prove inadequate, because of the strength and playfulness of a cockatoo, large earthenware dog bowls can be used.

Diet should be as recommended for Amazons, although many cockatoos will consume more greenfood (even stalks of cabbage, cauliflower and the stalk and centre from peppers). Much may be wasted, but they do enjoy shredding them. In addition, cockatoos should have nuts. The large species can crack whole Brazils and walnuts; the smaller ones enjoy cracked or halved nuts, and also pine nuts and peanuts.

Breeding cockatoos is a challenge. Sexing is easy in those species in which the male has a black iris and the female a brown or red-brown iris. A serious problem (more common in *galerita*, *sulphurea*, *ducorpsi* and *leadbeateri*) is that the male often attacks the female because she is not in breeding condition. Such attacks can be swift and fatal, sometimes resulting in the female's upper mandible being torn off. It can happen in long established, or newly introduced pairs. For this reason, it may be advisable to cut the male's flight feathers before introducing the female.

Unlike most male parrots, white cockatoos share incubation, usually carrying out this task during the day. The clutch consists of two to four eggs which are incubated for about twenty-eight days. The young

IDENTIFICATION OF WHITE COCKATOOS

SPECIES	APPROX LENGTH		BEAK	DISTINGUISHING FEATURES	ORIGIN
	cm	in			
Greater Sulphur-crested (*C. galerita galerita*)	54	21	black	yellow crest – narrow feathers	Australia
Triton (*C. g. triton*)	47	18	black	yellow crest – broader feathers	New Guinea, Indonesia
Blue-eyed (*C. ophthalmica*)	50	19	black	broad yellow crest feathers, brighter blue skin around eye	New Britain, New Ireland
✝ Lesser Sulphur-crested (*C. sulphurea sulphurea*)	33	12½	black	yellow crest – narrow feathers, ear coverts yellow	Indonesia, including Celebes, Sunda
✝ Timor (*C. s. parvula*)	30	12	black	smaller beak, slimmer body	Indonesia, including Djampea
✝ Citron-crested (*C. s. citrinocristata*)	34	13	black	orange crest – narrow feathers, faint orange ear coverts	Sunda, Indonesia
✝ Umbrella (White-crested) (*C. alba*)	46	18	black	white crest – very broad feathers	northern and central Indonesia
Moluccan (Salmon-crested) (*C. moluccensis*)	50	20	black	spectacular salmon crest, long, broad feathers	southern Moluccan Islands, Indonesia
Bare-eyed (Little Corella) (*C. sanguinea sanguinea* or *C. pastinator sanguinea*)	36	14	whitish-grey	grey-blue skin surrounding eye – more below; short white crest, orange-pink at base	northern Australia
Western Long-billed Corella (*C. pastinator pastinator* or *C. tenuirostris pastinator*)	39	16	whitish-grey	deep salmon feathers on forehead and lores, short white crest	south-western Australia
Slender-billed (*C. tenuirostris tenuirostris*)	39	16	whitish-grey	As in *pastinator*, but with salmon feathers on upper breast	south-eastern Australia
✝ Goffins's (*C. goffini*)	31	13	whitish-grey	short white crest, orange-pink at base of crest and on lores, circular white skin around eye	Tenimber Islands
✝ Philippine Red-vented (*C. haematuropygia*)	32	13	whitish-grey	under tail coverts red, short white crest	Philippine Islands
✝ Ducorp's (*C. ducorpsi*)	35	14	whitish-grey	white crest, broad feathers, blue skin around eye	Solomon Islands

There can be considerable size variation within a species.
✝ Male: iris black/female: iris brown or reddish-brown.

remain in the nest for ten, eleven, or sometimes twelve weeks. Animal protein should be included in the diet while the young are being reared.

The Roseate differs from other cockatoos in its short incubation period (twenty-three days) and in that its young leave the nest at seven weeks. The clutch size is usually two to four, but can be up to six.

CONSERVATION
The habitats of many parrot species, especially those occurring in rainforest, have been greatly reduced, even almost totally destroyed, in recent years. This applies particularly to those birds inhabiting islands (notably the Caribbean and certain Indonesian islands), south-eastern Brazil and many other areas of South and Central America, and other parts of the tropics where development has been rapid and recent. It applies not only to Third World countries but even to Australia where forests are destroyed to make way for agriculture. In New Guinea, for example, development is relatively recent, but will endanger the existence of many bird species within the next couple of decades. Some parrots can adapt to an altered habitat and live in agricultural areas or secondary forest, but many other species cannot and are doomed to extinction unless destruction of their habitat ceases.

For a number it is already too late. On the Indian Ocean island of Mauritius, the native Echo Parrakeet (*Psittacula eques*), found nowhere else, has already been reduced to the last dozen representatives of its species because it can live only in its native habitat, most of which was destroyed by the early 1970s. A belated programme was initiated to attempt to save it, but when the population of a species has been reduced to only double figures, such action is usually far too late.

In some instances captive breeding can play a very valuable part in conservation. Unfortunately, most highly endangered parrot species have too few representatives in captivity (or even none at all) for this to be possible. However, some Amazons, conures and *Cyanoramphus* parrakeets will almost certainly be saved from extinction by captive breeding.

It may be the case that there are already more examples of some species in captivity than in the wild. Certain Australian parrakeets, which are nomadic and inhabit the remote interior, are so little known that their current status cannot be recorded accurately. Thus, captive populations at least ensure the continued existence of the species, although many conservationists argue that multi-generation captive-breeding alters a species to the point where it is so far removed from its wild counterpart that it could not survive if reintroduced to the wild. Undoubtedly this is correct in some instances.

In other cases, however, captive-breeding over a short term can be used to increase the numbers of a threatened species quite rapidly. Only if suitable habitat existed could captive-bred birds be returned to the wild, but it is precisely because their habitat has been destroyed that they are endangered. In a few cases the combined pressures of trade and deforestation have caused the decline. In recent years international legislation (see *CITES*) has ensured that trade will no longer threaten the existence of species, but such legislation cannot be totally effective until signed and upheld by most countries throughout the world.

CONURE
Conure is the name given to certain genera of parrakeets from South and Central America. Members of the *Aratinga*, *Pyrrhura* and *Cyanoliseus* genera are invariably known as conures, whereas the two species of the genus *Enicognathus* can be known as either, for example, Slender-billed Conure or Slender-billed Parrakeet.

Conures have a reputation for being noisy and destructive. This is true of the larger species, but not of the *Pyrrhuras*. All are very interesting aviary birds, many are free-breeding and most make exceptionally good parents. Young birds make enchanting, affectionate and intelligent pets, their main drawback being that they shriek for attention in a voice that is far from pleasant.

See also: *Aratinga CONURES, Enicognathus CONURES, Nandayus CONURE,*

41

PATAGONIAN CONURE and *Pyrrhura CONURES.*

Coracopsis **PARROTS** – See *VASA PARROTS*

CRIMSON-WINGED PARRAKEETS (*Aprosmictus*)

The two parrakeets in this genus are distinctive birds of great beauty. They are mainly green with red in the wings. Their appearance is neat and the tail longish and broad. In length they are about 32 cm (13 in).

The Australian Crimson-wing (*A. erythropterus*) is well established in captivity and a favourite with many breeders. The male is an exceptionally handsome bird – and unmistakable, being the only parrakeet to have shining black on its back. The lower back is blue. The female is almost entirely green with a narrower area of red along the length of the wing.

In both sexes the beak is red in adults and yellowish in young birds. Immature birds resemble the female. Adult plumage is acquired during the third year, but males usually show some black feathers on the mantle at about eighteen months.

It is found in northern and eastern Australia, as far south as northern New South Wales, and in southern New Guinea. Its diet in the wild includes the seeds of eucalyptus and acacia, fruits, berries, nuts, insects and nectar.

Traditional, rather than suspended, aviaries are recommended. In length they should be in the region of 3.6–4.2 m (12–14 ft). When the young are due to fledge, they must be protected from flying at speed into the wire by placing a mass of branches at the end of the aviary. Crimson-wings greatly enjoy rain-bathing, so part of the roof should be of wire only.

A varied seed mixture should be offered, containing sunflower, safflower, canary, buckwheat, oats, white millet and, in cold weather, a little niger and linseed. Peanuts, small pine nuts and spray millet are relished. Fresh fruit and vegetables should be offered daily, especially chickweed, sowthistle, seeding grasses, spinach, celery and carrot, also apple and orange. Berries from hawthorn, elder and rowan are favourites, and some Crimson-wings will also eat blackberries.

They start to breed at three years. As they are often early nesters, the box should be in position by February. It should measure approximately 31 cm (12 in) square and 61 cm (2 ft) high. Some breeders have found that withholding the nest until, say, April, when the weather might be more favourable, has resulted in the birds not nesting at all. Three to six eggs are laid, but the number is usually four or five. The incubation period is twenty-one days.

Newly hatched chicks are thickly covered in white down which is replaced by grey down by the age of about ten days. By three weeks they are feathering up, with red and green wing feathers erupting. They leave the nest between five and six weeks.

Nest inspection should be carried out daily, as soon after first light as possible, especially with pairs which have not hatched chicks previously. The main danger is that the female ceases to brood the young at night, before they can maintain their body temperature. This is the principal reason for death in chicks found with food in their crops. If the nest is inspected early in the day there is a chance that chilled chicks can be saved. Males usually help to feed the chicks while in the nest.

A watch must be kept for signs of aggression in males which are trying to drive the female to nest. To prevent injury to the female, it may be necessary to clip the male's wings. The Crimson-wing may seem an unlikely subject for a colony aviary, yet, in the USA, one well-known aviculturist has an aviary containing six pairs; it measures 9 × 4.5 × 2.7 m high (30 × 15 × 9 ft). No serious fighting has occurred.

The Timor Crimson-winged Parrakeet (*A. jonquillaceus*) has less striking but more subtle coloration. A much lighter, more delicate shade of green, it has the mantle and upper back dark green. The male has the margins of these feathers in blue, and also the bend of the wing. The female lacks the blue margins and has the bend of the wing green. Some of the wing coverts are yellow, tinged with green. In the smaller sub-species *wetterensis*, these wing coverts are green, slightly suffused with yellow.

D

DIET

Diet, environment (including temperature), hygiene and avoidance of stress are the most important factors for a long and healthy life in captive parrots. Of these, diet is the most easily controlled, and careful attention must be paid to it. Variety in the diet is extremely important, and with some birds (especially wild-caught), it is often necessary to persevere for a long period, possibly several years, to achieve this. A bias towards one item of food, such as sunflower seed, can result in dietary deficiencies, obesity and even damage to internal organs such as the liver. If a bird's diet consisted of 60% sunflower seed or some other acceptable item of food, this would be unlikely to prove harmful provided that the other 40% consisted of a variety of foods, including fresh fruits and vegetables. These are an important source of Vitamins A and B which are essential for good health. (See also *SEED, SUNFLOWER*.)

The diet of many species can include items from the table which, if sensibly chosen, are nourishing and beneficial. Owners should not worry unduly if their pets prefer to eat cooked meat and vegetables, rice, pasta, bread, crackers and other biscuits and cakes. They could live on this indefinitely and be a lot healthier than a parrot which had to exist solely on dry seed.

It is very important to experiment, because no two parrots have the same preferences where food is concerned. There are some items which are almost universally popular (except with small species), such as cracked walnuts, hawthorn berries, corn on the cob, grapes and pomegranates, and few birds, whatever their size, will refuse spray millet.

In addition to variety, an obviously important aspect of correct feeding is the suitability of the items offered. It is no good giving Pesquet's Parrots seed, macaws nectar, or lories nuts. Whereas many species are omnivorous, others are specialist feeders and *must* have the correct food if they are to survive. In my opinion, parrots should have food in front of them at all times: they should not be rationed. Neither should the diet consist largely of manufactured foods, such as pellets. These are very satisfactory for poultry, but not for parrots, whose enjoyment of foods of different types, textures and flavours should be supremely evident to any caring owner. They receive no enjoyment – and incidentally no essential wear on the beak – from such artificial fare.

See also *FRUITS, GRIT, NECTAR, PROTEIN* and *VEGETABLES*.

DUSKY LORY– see *Pseudeos LORY*

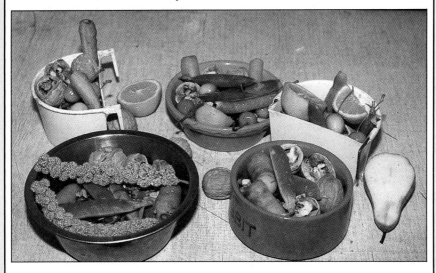

Aim for variety in the diet, especially with fresh fruits and vegetables.

E

ECLECTUS PARROTS

Eclectus have three great assets which have assured their popularity as aviary birds: they are spectacularly colourful, sexually dimorphic (they can be sexed at three and a half weeks old!), and nest readily. They originate from Australia, New Guinea and Indonesia, although most of those now available are captive-bred.

An Eclectus chick.

There is only one species of Eclectus, but recognition of the seven sub-species is difficult in the males, which do not differ greatly. The main differences are in length (31–38 cm/12–15 in), in shade of green, and whether or not the tail is tipped with yellow.

Females differ significantly, and the principal features used for recognition are as follows:

1 A narrow circle of blue feathers surrounding the eye, as in the Red-sided (*E. r. polychloros*), *E. r. macgillivrayi* from northern Australia, which is not likely to be encountered outside that country, and in the smallest race, *solomonensis*, which is not common in captivity.

2 Absence of blue on the underparts (all red) as in *cornelia* and the larger *riedeli*.

3 Yellow in the tail and lacking blue feathers around the eye, as in the nominate race and *vosmaeri*, two of the larger sub-species.

Immature birds can be distinguished by the greyish iris and by the bill colour which is brownish.

Eclectus have long been among my own favourites. Many become very tame and even aviary birds will mimic sounds around them, including a few words. Young ones readily learn to talk, some even without tuition. However, the females tend to be bad tempered and definitely cannot be recommended as pets. Breeding pairs can be kept in suspended cages or traditional aviaries.

The measurements of the nest-box should be about 31 cm (12 in) square and 61 cm (2 ft) high. In some pairs females are dominant and could keep the male away from the food; two feeding points should be provided if there is any hint of this, especially in newly introduced birds.

It is quite usual for families to spend most of their lives inside the nest once they are sexually mature. One clutch follows another, within about three weeks if the first was not successful, or after removal of the young. The two eggs are incubated for twenty-eight days and the young spend ten to eleven weeks in the nest.

An abundance of fresh vegetables and fruits, and also berries such as hawthorn and elder, is very important. Deprived of sufficient Vitamin A, Eclectus will contract candidiasis (lesions may be seen in the mouth). Carrots and tomatoes are good sources of this vitamin, or a multi-vitamin additive (most of which have a high Vitamin A content) may be added to a favourite item of food, or to bread and milk.

Most Eclectus will eat many small seeds, such as white millet, canary and hemp, in addition to sunflower and safflower, spray millet, peanuts and pine nuts. Celery, cubes of cheese and corn on the cob are favoured items.

Some Eclectus can be very noisy – enough to disturb neighbours – but individuals vary considerably in this respect.

A newly hatched Salvadori's Fig Parrot (*Psittaculirostris salvadorii*).

females.) The shell is secreted from a gland in the uterus. The shell of a fertile egg becomes thinner during the incubation period because the chick draws on the calcium it contains for its own skeletal growth. A thin-shelled egg is therefore unlikely to produce a viable chick. It may also cause the female to become eggbound.

The range of size and weight in parrot eggs is obviously great. In the Spectacled Parrotlet (*Forpus conspicillatus*), for example, a female weighs about 25 g, and the new-laid egg weighs about 1 g and measures approximately 16 × 15 mm (⅝ in). In a Moluccan Cockatoo, the adult weighs about 800 g (28 oz), the egg weighs about 25 g and measures 44 × 32 mm (1.7 × 1.2 in). Young birds, laying for the first time, and old birds tend to lay smaller eggs than those of optimum breeding age.

See also *CLUTCH*.

EGGS

All parrot eggs are white, as is usual in hole-nesting birds. Their shape varies according to species, individual females and even among eggs in the same clutch. Published sizes for eggs should be used only as an approximate guide, as variation is so great. Most parrot eggs are ovoid (oval with one end more pointed than the other). The purpose of this shape is that when the narrow ends are pointing inwards, the eggs are more compact, thus reducing the area which the incubating bird has to cover, and minimising heat loss.

The components of the egg are the yolk (which provides the nutrition for the growing embryo), the albumen or egg-white (an albuminous sac and liquid albumen, which protect the yolk), the germinal spot from which the embryo will develop, and the membranes. There are two layers of the latter, separated at the blunt end to form an air space. Before hatching, the chick ruptures this membrane with its egg tooth and breathes in the air. The function of the air space is to conserve the limited water supply of the embryo by re-condensing respiratory moisture.

The outer layer of the egg is the shell, which consists of about 94% calcium carbonate. (It can thus be seen why calcium is of vital importance in the diet of breeding

Enicognathus CONURES

This genus of South American parrakeets contains two species: the Slender-billed Conure (*E. leptorhynchus*) and the Austral Conure (*E. ferruginea*). The former is unmistakable because it possesses a very long narrow beak.

Both species have long tails and green plumage, most of the feathers being margined with black or dusky-grey. The forehead and lores are brownish-red (the feathers having a slightly dense, bushy appearance in the Slender-billed). There are some maroon feathers, or a maroon patch on the abdomen.

The length is about 35 cm (14 in) in the nominate race of the Austral and about 31 cm (12 in) in the sub-species *minor*, the one usually seen in captivity.

The Slender-billed is a larger bird, of about 41 cm (16 in); the tail accounts for about 17 cm (7 in) of this length. Young Slender-bills have the beak shorter and the bare skin surrounding the eye white (it is grey in adults).

The Austral Conure is not a tropical species, like most other parrots; indeed, it has the most southerly distribution of any member of the family, being found in Tierra del Fuego in Chile, and ranging as far north as south-western Argentina. Not surprisingly, the plumage of this

A parent-reared Slender-billed Conure (*Enicognathus leptorhynchus*), aged thirty-four days, weighing 284 g (10 oz). The long bill of the adult is not yet apparent.

species is dense. This thick feathering is utilised in display, when the feathers of the head are 'puffed' out to make the bird look larger than it is.

It occurs in forested areas and is associated with *Nothofagus* beech trees. It usually nests in hollows in the trees, but one ornithologist has recorded that if such holes are not available, a nest will be built, using twigs or grass stems, among the foliage of the bamboo-like *Chusquea*.

Four to eight eggs are laid, and the incubation period is about twenty-five days.

This species seems to be naturally tame and inquisitive. My own birds delight in nipping fingers at feeding time. One, which I kept as a pet when he was the only one of his species in the UK, proved amazingly obedient. When I called him he would fly to my shoulder to be returned to his cage. Once inside he would roll over to be tickled, something few parrots permit, yet he would never allow me to scratch his head.

My birds are passionately fond of the strong-tasting buds of lombardy poplar. When bunches are placed in the aviary, they spend hours eating the buds and stripping the bark.

The Slender-billed Conure is found in Chile, where it is declining because of the clearing of forest, excessive hunting and, apparently, in recent years,

Newcastle disease. This species feeds on the ground (on roots), as well as in trees, on seeds and nuts (especially seeds from the cones of the pine *Araucaria araucana*).

Slender-bills are not popular with farmers, because of their habit of attacking cultivated crops, such as apples. Anyone who has seen one tear an apple apart to reach the pips, can be left in no doubt as to the damage they could cause. After cutting up apples I always give any loose pips to Slender-bills and Australs. After doing this for some years I read that apple pips are poisonous! It would be interesting to know on what evidence this statement was based.

Slender-bills will breed when only two years old. A female in my possession laid fertile eggs only eighteen days after the male was introduced; the clutch consisted of five eggs. Newly hatched chicks weigh about 11 g. Like most conures, Slender-bills are excellent parents and feed enormous amounts to their young. Weight gains of a parent-reared chick were as follows:

day 4,   20 g;
day 10, 57 g;
day 11, 78 g (eyes open),
day 12, 92 g (ears open),
day 14, 106 g;
day 16, 130 g;
day 18, 152 g;
day 24, 220 g (adult weight).

Rearing foods consisted of sprouted mung beans, sweetcorn

(thawed frozen kernels – whole fresh corn on the cob would have been better if available), wholemeal bread and milk with a powdered calcium and Vitamin D3 supplement, and soaked sunflower seed. Smaller quantities of celery, peas and apple were taken. When blackberries ripened, these were consumed with great eagerness. Slender-bills are also passionately fond of hawthorn berries. The young leave the nest at about seven and a half weeks old.

Owners of this species should note that they must have a deep container for drinking water; they have an unusual method of drinking which involves tipping the head right back.

Eolophus **COCKATOO** – see under *COCKATOOS*

Eos **LORIES**
Members of this genus are predominantly red, and small to medium in size – 23–31 cm (9–12 in). The bill is orange. They occur on various islands of New Guinea and Indonesia. The best known is undoubtedly the Red Lory (*Eos bornea*) which is almost entirely red, with some blue and black on the wings and under tail coverts. Free-breeding, yet beautiful, it is an ideal species for beginners with lories. However, it is prone to feather plucking and to plucking its young.

The diet is similar to that described for the *Chalcopsitta* lories, but members of this genus are more willing to try a variety of items, including greenfood.

As with all *Eos* species, two eggs are laid and incubated for about twenty-four days by the female. The young spend nine weeks or more in the nest. Immature birds have many feathers with dark tips, thus giving a mottled appearance.

The least typical member of the genus is the beautiful Blue-streaked (*E. reticulata*) from the Tenimber Islands in Indonesia, where its numbers must now have declined due to severe deforestation in the area. It has a longer tail than other *Eos*, and also pronounced blue shaft-streaked feathers on the neck; if it had bare skin surrounding the lower mandible it would surely have been classified as a *Chalcopsitta*.

Probably the most free-breeding member of the genus is the smallest species, the Violet-necked or Violet-naped Lory (*E. squamata*) from the western Papuan Islands. Its red plumage is irregularly marked with dull purple on the abdomen and neck. Some pairs are continuous breeders and will produce eight or more young a year if the chicks are removed for hand-rearing at an early age. This becomes essential if they are badly plucked, as so often happens.

Eunymphicus **PARRAKEETS**
The two beautiful and unusual crested parrakeets which form this genus are generally considered as sub-species. In the opinion of one, of perhaps only three or four aviculturists, who has extensive experience of both, they should be classified as separate species.

Their plumage differs little, apart from head coloration. The Horned Parrakeet (*E. cornutus cornutus*) is the more colourful, with its bright red forehead and crown, and yellow on its nape. The Uvaean Parrakeet (*E. c. uvaeensis*) lacks the yellow, and also the red tip to the crest feathers, and has only a small area of red on the forehead. Its beak is noticeably larger. The orange-red iris is striking in both birds, partly because of the contrast with the jet black feathers surrounding it.

In young birds the face is greyish, not black, and this area is reduced. The feathers of the forehead are black tipped with red. In the nominate race, the ear coverts are pale green instead of yellow. The bill is horn-coloured and the iris is brownish.

The Horned Parrakeet is found on the volcanic island of New Caledonia in the western Pacific. This forms an area of about 18,650 sq km (7,200 sq miles). The stronghold of this species is the Haute Yate Reserve – but it has declined here because of the destruction of its habitat.

In contrast, the Uvaean Parrakeet occurs only on Ouvea, one of the Loyalty Islands, a dependency of New Caledonia. Because of its tiny area of distribution, this is one of the most vulnerable of all parrots. Its range is only 4 or 5 km (2½–3 miles) in extent. Among parrots, only the Cayman Brac Amazon (*Amazona leucocephala hesterna*) has a

47

similarly small area of distribution.

The population of *uvaeensis* is believed to number in the region of 200, having declined due to deforestation and the further destruction of the forests by fire.

The *Eunymphicus* are intriguing birds – beautiful, intelligent and very quick on the wing. Loro Parque is probably the only place where both species can be seen side by side; here a pair of Horned Parrakeets are housed next to two male Uvaean. The latter are more timid, generally retreating to the depth of their 9 m (29 ft) long aviary, whereas the Horned are tamer and more inquisitive. Both are strong and agile in flight.

Horned Parrakeets are being bred in a few collections in Germany and Switzerland, and in one collection in France, since the 1970s. Three or four eggs are laid and incubated for about twenty-two days. The young spend five or six weeks in the nest. These birds have a marked need for animal protein when rearing young, and will consume mealworms, meat and cheese.

This species remains rare and expensive, but is gradually being established.

EXHIBITING

All shows that are staged for cage birds of every type have classes for parrots and other members of the parrot family. Generally, however, these are not well supported. Those who keep parrots in aviaries are seldom prepared to move them to a show hall, especially as shows are normally staged at the coldest time of the year. The species seen at shows are generally those kept by fanciers, i.e. people who breed for show or colour, and these are likely to be lovebirds, cockatiels and Grass Parrakeets (*Neophemas*) mainly, plus the pet parrots of the club members.

It is permitted to exhibit large parrots in the cages in which they are kept, whereas others must be staged in proper show cages. Although there are no standard sizes, the cages must conform to the usual pattern and be painted white inside and black outside.

The intending exhibitor should be familiar with the way the birds are staged and should visit a show or consult an experienced exhibitor. Enough food should be placed in the cage to last for the duration of the show. Special items, such as spray millet or fruit, can be given by the exhibitor *after* judging.

What does the judge look for? Primarily, perfect feather condition, but the bird must show itself well for this to be evident. It must be steady and at ease in the cage. Rarity of species should be considered only after these points have been taken into account.

Some of the larger shows have classes for talking birds, in which case the entries are judged solely on their talking ability. This class can draw the largest crowd, as people love to be entertained by talking birds.

For further details contact The Parrot Society, 19a De Parys Ave, Bedford, England.

Talented mimics such as Grey Parrots are a great attraction at shows that include classes for talkers.

F

FEATHER

Several different types of feathers are found in parrots. All birds have *contour feathers*, that is, the external feathers which, in parrots, are so much admired for their colours. In parrots these grow from tracts of skin (called pterylae): the areas between these (apteria) are actually bare. This is not apparent unless one parts the feathers, because all areas are covered by overlapping feathers. One can, for example, part the feathers on an Amazon's neck to reveal comparatively large bare areas.

The feather tracts have different arrangements in different species. These can be seen most easily in chicks just before the feathers start to erupt.

Parrots also possess *down feathers*, which grow from the skin of all parts of the body except the neck. These have a fluffy texture, and are not tightly knit like the contour feathers. The colour of down varies in different species, but is usually white, pale yellow or grey. In some Amazons, the newly opened down feathers are yellow, but soon fade to white.

Density of down also varies; species from high altitudes naturally have denser down than lowland birds. In chicks there are two kinds of down: the *natal down* (of newly hatched chicks) which is a very simple type, and the *second down*, which appears in most parrot species at between about ten and twenty days.

A third type of feather is the *powder down* – a modified down feather which is believed to grow throughout the life of the bird. The barbs of this feather disintegrate to produce a fine powder which is used for cleaning the feathers. This is more evident in some species than in others. Cockatoos, for example, give off clouds of dust from their powder down feathers; this should be borne in mind by anyone with allergies or chest complaints. The dust will be less of a nuisance in a pet bird if it is sprayed daily with warm water.

A few parrots also have *bristles* (more commonly found in softbill species, such as barbets, and also in pigeons). These are actually contour feathers which lack the barbs (the fine filaments attached to the central shaft). Bristles were apparent around the eyes and cere of a young Lesser Vasa Parrot (hand-reared and therefore tolerant of close examination). The eyelashes of parrots (more prominent in some species than others) are the same type of feather.

The range of colours found in members of the parrot family is surely more diverse than in any other group of birds. Plumage coloration and markings are extremely varied within the different genera. They could be placed in categories according to the continent from which they originate. Given a single parrot feather, someone with a good knowledge of parrots could tell you whether the owner of that feather originated from South America or from Australia, for example, even if he or she could not name the species.

In parrot feathers, there are two types of colours: structural and pigmentary. A feather consists of a central shaft to which the barbs are attached. Each barb has two rows of sidebranches, the *barbules*. The components responsible for structural colour are present in the barbs and barbules. Some colours are due principally to the back-scattering of light from the many hollow keratin cylinders which make up the spongy structure of the barbs. Iridescent colours are believed to result from barbules which are flattened for part of their length and twisted at right angles.

The other factor responsible for feather colour is pigment. There are a number of types of pigment, the most common of which is melanin, while another type is carotenoid. There are also others of unknown composition. Colour in parrot feathers can also be the result of the combination of pigmentary and structural colours.

A wonderful range of colours may be found in one feather. In the feathers of neotropical species, for example, the upper and lower surface of the feather has different coloration. In some feathers, the

A pair of
Citron-crested
Cockatoos *(Cacatua
sulphurea
citrinocristata)*. The
difference in eye
colour is obvious in
male and female.

Cockatoos (2)

A captive-bred Banksian, or Red-tailed Black Cockatoo *(Calyptorhynchus magnificus)*.

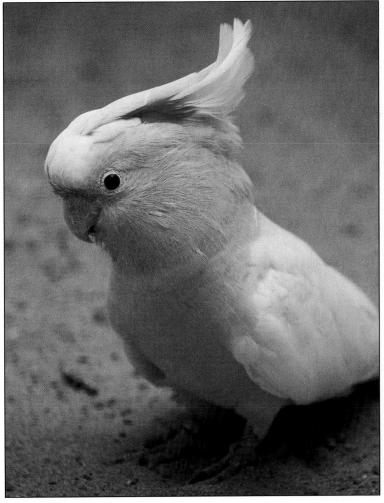

Leadbeater's Cockatoo *(Cacatua leadbeateri)* – usually considered the most beautiful of the white cockatoos.

manner in which one colour fades into another is remarkably subtle; in others the colours are sharply divided.

FEATHER PLUCKING

Nearly all cases of self feather mutilation are due to some form of stress. This includes the unfulfilled desire to breed which is so common in parrots kept on their own. As soon as the problem becomes evident, it is important to try to find the cause. In some cases, notably Grey Parrots, it can be so severe and so rapid that the main hope of curing the problem, i.e. pairing the bird up for breeding, is ruled out because a badly plucked bird cannot be kept out of doors, behave normally or incubate efficiently.

Certain parrots of a nervous temperament are very prone to the problem: Queen of Bavaria's Conures, Red-fronted Macaws and Gang Gang Cockatoos are notorious. Keeping them supplied daily with fresh branches may help. Sometimes they regrow all their feathers and look superb – then, in a couple of hours, they denude themselves completely again, in response to some form of stress. Some pet Grey Parrots, for example, are so easily stressed that

Feather plucking is very common in Grey Parrots (Psittacus erithacus erithacus). It usually begins with a few feathers being removed from the breast.

any alteration to the cage or its position can cause this behaviour.

Feather plucking is rarely the result of incorrect feeding or feather mites, as is sometimes suggested. It could be caused by irritated dry skin, however, and this is one reason why regular spraying is so important.

Many cases of plucking first occur when a single bird reaches sexual maturity, being an indication that it needs a mate. However, many birds, such as lovebirds and cockatiels, will also pluck their mates or their young. On removing the young birds when they are independent, the feathers usually grow in a few weeks. All in all, feather plucking is usually a difficult problem to deal with; one has to try to understand the psychology of the bird in order to rectify the cause where self-plucking is concerned. (See *STRESS*.)

FERAL PARROTS

Feral populations are those which establish themselves outside their native habitat. They are derived from escaped or released cage birds. Certain species are remarkable for their ability to thrive in almost any habitat and, with a little help in the way of food, any climate. The Indian Ringneck Parrakeet, for example, can be found in small groups in several areas of England, aided by winter feeding. A few breeding successes may occur, but the groups have always remained small.

On the other hand, in more favourable climates the species can multiply to the degree that it becomes an agricultural pest. It may even occupy the niche once held by an extinct species or a species which is extinct in the area. In Puerto Rico, for example, where the native parrot is now confined to the Luquillo Mountains, the Hispaniolan Amazon (from the neighbouring Dominican Republic which consists of Haiti and San Domingo) is fairly well established in the lowlands. Other smaller parrots, such as *Aratinga* conures from South America, are also breeding there.

An introduced species can pose a very serious threat to an endangered species. On the island of Mauritius in the Indian Ocean, the introduced Indian Ringneck could become a nest competitor against the critically endangered Echo Parrakeet (*Psittacula eques*), of which only about a dozen are known to survive.

Feral species are usually those which are already widespread and numerous in their country of origin because they are able to adapt themselves to a wide variety of habitats. This is true of the Ringneck Parrakeet. Or they may have established themselves because their adopted country has many similarities to their native country.

In South Florida, there are thriving feral populations of parrots and parrakeets from South America (also mynahs from Asia). In December 1987, I visited the roosting site of one such flock. Located a few feet from a busy road, the site was a small stand of casuarina trees by an apartment building. Across the street was a park containing plenty of trees, making one wonder why this particular stand was so attractive to the parrots.

FIG PARROTS (*Opopsitta* and *Psittaculirostris*)

The small and extremely beautiful Fig Parrots are difficult subjects in captivity. Very rarely imported until the early 1970s, much remains to be learned about them, as captive breeding has succeeded only rarely. Active, quiet and fascinating to observe, they are among the most attractive aviary birds imaginable.

The *Psittaculirostris* species originate from New Guinea. They measure about 18 cm (7 in). The smaller *Opopsitta* (13–14 cm/about 5 in) are found in New Guinea, Australia and the Aru Islands of Indonesia.

Sexual dimorphism is marked or absent. All have large heads, strong bills and very short pointed tails.

The diet must contain large quantities of fruit, including dried figs which should be soaked in water overnight. Each bird should be offered at least three figs daily, or more if small ones are used. A Vitamin K supplement (either drops or crushed tablets) should be added to the figs two or three times a week. Without this vitamin, laying females may haemorrhage

and other distressing problems may occur.

Apple, pear, grapes and cactus fruits are relished, and some Fig Parrots will also eat banana and pomegranate. A seed mixture containing sunflower and various small seeds should always be available, and spray millet is relished.

Fresh branches for gnawing are essential if the beak is not to become overgrown. If these are not available, the aviary woodwork and perches will be attacked. Like lories, these birds need a nest-box

Orange-breasted Fig Parrots of two different sub-species: *Opopsitta gulielmi nigrifons* and, second from right, *O.g. amabilis.*

to retire to at night or when danger threatens.

There are two species of *Opopsitta*, the Double-eyed (*O. diophthalma*) which is rare in captivity, and the Orange-breasted (*O. gulielmiterti*) which is extremely rare. The Double-eyed is green with the forehead red and a touch of skyblue above the eye. The cheeks are red in the male and whitish in the female. This species is difficult to establish when newly imported; even acclimatised birds should not be subjected to temperatures lower than 10°C (50°F).

The clutch consists of two eggs which are incubated for eighteen to twenty days. In one carefully documented record of captive breeding, a young bird left the nest at fifty-two days; in another, the single youngster spent about thirty-nine days in the nest.

The three species of *Psittaculirostris* are among my own favourite parrots. Salvadori's (*P. salvadorii*) has the feathers of its cheeks (yellow in the male and greenish-yellow in the female) elongated and standing away from the head. The male has the upper breast red, this area being bluish-green in the female.

Cockatoos (3)

The Philippine, or Red-vented Cockatoo *(Cacatua haematuropygia)* is not frequently available.

A Palm Cockatoo *(Probosciger aterrimus)* – a magnificent bird from New Guinea.

The White-tailed
Black Cockatoo
(*Calyptorhynchus
funereus baudinii*) is
rare in captivity and
declining in the wild.

Desmarest's (*P. desmarestii*) is an extremely beautiful bird with a scarlet forehead and golden-orange on the crown and nape; below the eye is a small patch of brilliant blue. The area below the throat is skyblue and vinous in the nominate race, in which male and female are alike.

In the sub-species *godmani*, the male has the hind-neck yellow, but the female lacks this.

Edwards' (*P. edwardsii*) is easily distinguished by its dark red cheeks, the feathers of which are elongated, as are those of the bright yellow ear coverts. In the male the breast is dark red, in the female it is yellow-green.

Any breeding success can be classed as an achievement. I personally believe that animal protein in the diet, such as mealworms, greatly increases the chance of a chick being reared. A Salvadori's hatched at Loro Parque thrived until the age of six weeks, when, sadly, it died of enteritis: for the first three or four weeks the parents consumed at least 100 mealworms daily. In later clutches, when mealworms were not available (in hot weather it is impossible to keep and feed them because they are attacked by ants), chicks, which hatched on three occasions, survived less than a week.

These Fig Parrots lay two eggs, which are incubated by the female for about twenty-four days. The young leave the nest after eight weeks. They can be kept in colonies.

FOOT
There are several different toe formations in birds, that of parrots being zygodactyl, that is, two toes point forwards and two point backwards. The curved claws provide a strong grip and the toenails are quite sharp in the larger species (agonisingly so in some very young birds, such as Grey Parrots). The foot is covered in scales, reminiscent of snake skin. This skin is probably moulted once a year (certainly the case in my pet Yellow-fronted Amazon).

Many genera of parrots (such as *Amazona*, *Cacatua*, *Calyptorhynchus* and *Poicephalus*) use a foot to hold food; it is a very efficient grasping tool. Some also use the foot in defence (such as *Ara* and *Amazona*) when perched; in the nest they will turn over on their backs and strike upwards with the feet (*Ara*). Nestlings will do this instinctively. Many parrots, especially those mentioned above, use a foot to scratch their heads.

FORCE-FEEDING
At times force-feeding is essential if a bird's life is to be saved. It may cease to feed itself because it is sick or severely stressed, or because it is a recently captured wild bird. Force-feeding may also be necessary to ensure that a bird is receiving sufficient food, or more nutritious food than that which it chooses. Most young birds can be spoon-fed unless removed from the nest near to the age of fledging.

Force-feeding is accomplished with the aid of a syringe. Most pharmacies sell plastic, disposable syringes which are ideal for the purpose after the needle has been discarded. A length of plastic tubing, of a suitable size for the bird concerned, is attached to the syringe. The food used could consist of high protein baby cereal, a vitamin and mineral supplement and Ringer's lactate (a physiological solution containing various salts and minerals, obtainable from a veterinarian), or water, preferably distilled or mineral (non-carbonated).

The food must be of a suitable consistency to flow through the syringe. If additional items to those

The toe formation in parrots is zygodactyl, that is, two toes point forward and two backward.

suggested above are used, they must be blended very well to ensure that there are no lumps in the food. There is nothing more frustrating then having a syringe blocked by a small bit of food.

The syringe should be prepared by lubricating the leading edge of the inner part with petroleum jelly to ensure it moves freely. When filled, it should be turned upside down and depressed a little to dispel any air. The plastic tube should be dipped into hot water before being placed in the bird's mouth, to ensure that it is warm and slides easily into the crop. (The food must, of course, also have been heated, then stirred well to ensure there are no hot spots.)

The tube should be inserted down the right side of the bird's throat. The syringe is then slowly depressed to release the food. In the case of a large and powerful parrot, such as a macaw, it is advisable for two people to carry out the task of force-feeding. One holds the bird steady and also holds the top of the plastic tube on the syringe. The force of the pumping action of the bird could result in the tube losing contact with the syringe and the bird swallowing the tube.

Great care must be taken to ensure that the tube enters the crop (which it is almost certain to do if directed to the right side of the throat). If food were to enter the lungs, the bird would drown instantly.

Forpus PARROTLETS – see *PARROTLETS* (**Forpus**)

FRACTURES

If your bird breaks a leg or a wing, do not panic. You will need to seek the advice of a veterinarian who is used to handling birds, but, in the meantime, keep the patient warm, using a heat lamp if necessary. Keep the bird as inactive as possible. A glass-fronted aquarium or brooder is ideal for this purpose, because the bird is unable to climb about. As a temporary measure, a cardboard box will suffice for smaller birds.

A veterinarian can advise one of three courses of action: surgery, fixing the limb externally (by means of a splint, for example), or simply trying to keep the bird as inactive as possible.

There are several factors to be considered. Not all vets have the necessary experience with birds to operate on them. Surgery is usually more expensive, but healing is generally more rapid than with other methods. Surgery is not usually practicable for small birds.

Not all birds will tolerate a splint; an Elizabethan collar may have to be put around the bird's neck to prevent it removing the splint – and this could be the cause of more stress. One danger of a splint is that the bandage holding it in place may be applied too tightly, resulting in the blood supply to the limb being cut off. The patient then loses all sensation in that area and may bite off the limb. This is what happened to a Jendaya Conure whose leg splint was bound too tightly. After three or four days it chewed its leg off. (Fortunately it was young and quickly adapted to its disability.)

It may be necessary to delay treatment for a bird suffering from shock, until it has recovered from the initial stress. On the other hand, many cases of broken legs need urgent attention.

In an emergency a leg splint can be made from a small plastic syringe cut in half lengthways, or from a piece of lightweight aluminium shaped to the leg. Cotton wool should be placed between it and the tape used to bind it to the leg. A broken wing can also be taped to the body – but not so tightly that it constricts the chest, which could result in suffocation. However, broken limbs should always be attended to by a veterinarian, who may have the facilities to X-ray the patient. This will reveal whether the bone is infected – a serious condition known as osteomyelitis. Some bones communicate with the air sacs, and thus infections can result from external contamination.

Chicks with fractures can be treated in the same way. Splints and bandages can be very stressful to chicks at first, although they generally tolerate them quite well after a while. A broken leg can be mended perfectly after two weeks. During this period the diet should include a calcium/Vitamin D3 supplement. Chicks suffering from rickets, due to lack of calcium, are a tragic sight, possibly with several fractures of the legs and/or wings.

Lories (1)

The Tahiti Blue Lory *(Vini peruviana)*, found on a few small islands of the Pacific, is declining in the wild and an extreme rarity in captivity.

The most readily available of the *Lorius* lories, the Chattering Lory *(Lorius garrulus garrulus)*, is a delightful aviary bird.

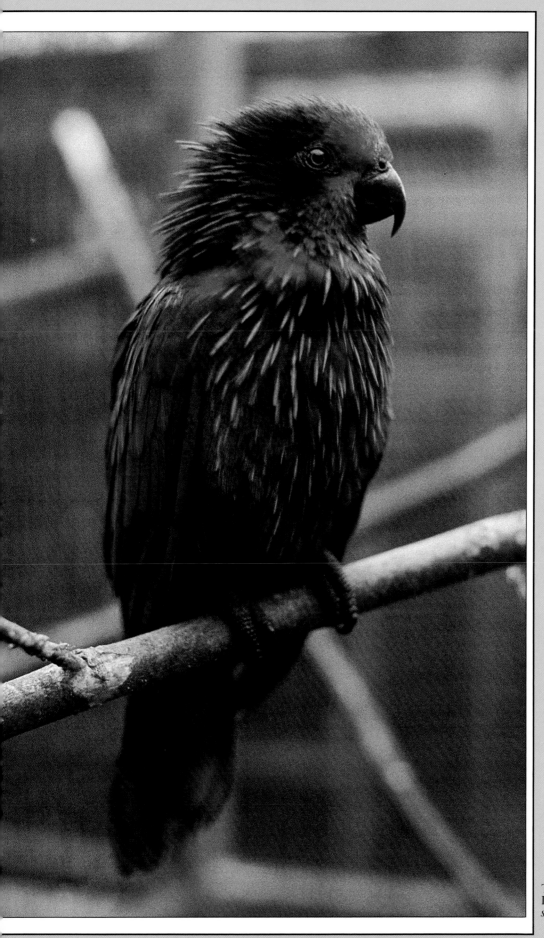

The Yellow-streaked
Lory *(Chalcopsitta
scintillata)*.

Usually there is no option but to destroy them – a sad waste of young life and a distressing experience which could so easily have been avoided.

FRENCH MOULT

This is the term given to malformation and loss of the flight and tail feathers in birds in nest feather. The degree of severity varies; in some cases the feathers are replaced by normal ones, but in many instances the replacement feathers are poorly formed (with blood remaining in the quill) or soon drop out, and thus the bird is never able to fly. French moult is best known, and has been extensively studied, in budgerigars but it could occur in any psittacine species. It is not confined solely to birds in captivity, but has been recorded in the wild in a number of species of Australian parrots.

There are numerous theories regarding the cause of French moult, none of which have been proved conclusively. However, it seems likely that a number of factors are to blame. A virus is most likely, especially papovavirus, also known as budgerigar fledgling disease.

It should be noted that, in Australia, the term French moult is used for psittacine beak and feather disease (*PBFDS*).

Missing tail and flight feathers indicate that this young budgerigar is suffering from French moult.

FRUITS

Newcomers to parrot keeping are often cautious in their choice of fruits; they may even withhold fruit totally because it makes their parrot's faeces loose. However, loose droppings are only a cause for concern when the diet consists almost entirely of hard seeds (highly unnatural), not when it contains soft items on a daily basis.

Fruit should not be rationed. Few species, except those that require large amounts, such as Hawk-headed Parrots and caiques, will eat excessive quantities.

It is difficult to persuade many wild-caught imported parrots to eat fruit. Perseverance over a long period may be necessary. Where possible, a bird which refuses fruit should be kept near, or with one which relishes it.

Apples   These are perhaps the most widely fed fruits and among the most popular. However, there are over 2,000 varieties, not all of which are eaten with equal relish. Golden Delicious and Cox's are favourites of many. They can be fed cut into slices, or, for small species, half an apple can be spiked onto a nail on the perch.

Apricots   These would be an excellent food for parrots if one could persuade them to eat them. They retain their high Vitamin A content even when cooked, dried or tinned, and many parrots suffer diseases because their diet is deficient in Vitamin A. The carotene content of apricots is also very high.

Avocado   is poisonous to parrots. Do not feed it.

Bananas   The liking for this fruit appears to be very much an individual taste where parrots are concerned. Some lories and macaws will eat large quantities, but parrakeets ignore this fruit.

Blackberry (Rubus fruticosus)   The European blackberry is relished by some parrots and ignored by others. (In my own collection Iris Lorikeets and Eclectus Parrots adore them for the small pips or seeds that they contain.)

Cherry (sweet)   This is a great favourite of many of the larger species, especially those with a bill strong enough to crack the kernel, which is apparently considered a great delicacy. The flesh may be eaten or discarded in the haste to reach the stone. It should be noted that the leaves of the wild cherry are said to be poisonous.

Elderberry (*Sambucus nigra*) (*European black elder*)   The berries are an excellent food for parrots, enjoyed by many species. During an autumn when they are plentiful, it is worth freezing some. Fresh berries contain a small quantity of the amino acid tyrosin.

Fig   A natural food for many species. However (expensive) fresh figs were untouched by my parrots, whereas dried figs, which have been soaked in water overnight, are highly favoured by certain species. Fig Parrots (*Psittaculirostris* and *Opopsitta*) should receive at least two each daily.

Grapes   Table grapes are relished by all the larger parrots and by some of the small ones. Some birds will discard the fruit to reach the pips which are highly favoured.

Kiwifruit   An excellent food if parrots will eat it. The content of potassium, calcium, magnesium and Vitamin C is high.

Mango   Juicy and fleshy when ripe, they are difficult to cut. Where it is grown locally, it is worth feeding; imported mangoes are expensive. Their nutritional value is high: mangoes contain large amounts of carotene, minerals (including potassium) and Vitamin C.

Nectarine   This mutant of the peach, which has firmer flesh, is a good food for any parrot that will eat it, being a fine source of carotene and potassium.

Orange   Many parrots, especially lories and the larger South American species, relish oranges. Generally, the best way to feed an orange is to leave the skin intact and to cut the orange into pieces, or into halves for lories and other birds which like to dig into fruit. Usually the rough-skinned varieties are preferred to those with smooth skins. Juicy mandarins, clementines and tangerines are also enjoyed. Some oranges are treated with fungicides and pesticides so the skins should be scrubbed in warm water to remove these. This is especially important for those birds which chew up, and probably eat, some of the skin.

Palm Fruits   Many parrots enjoy the fruits of palm trees, such as those of the Queen's Palm (*Arecastrum romanzoffianum*). At Loro Parque in Tenerife, where this palm grows freely, species as small as parrotlets (*Forpus*) and as large as macaws, relish them. Amazons and the larger *Psittacula* parrakeets are especially fond of them. The fruits are orange, round and about 2.5 cm (1 in) long, with a fibrous exterior and a very hard stone inside, which no bird can crack.

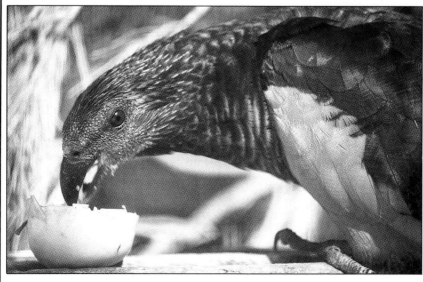

A Pesquet's Parrot (*Psittrichas fulgidus*) scooping out the flesh from an apple.

Lories (2)

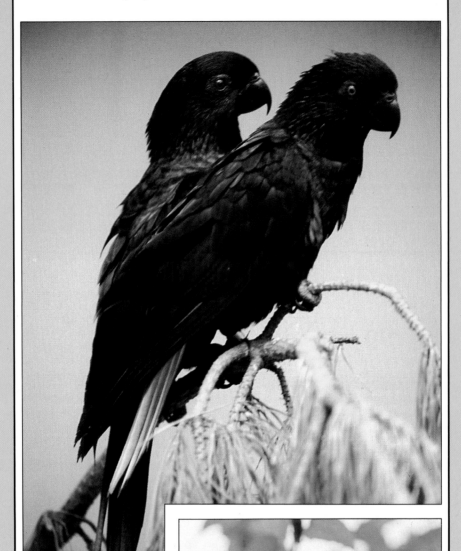

Black Lories
(Chalcopsitta atra)
from New Guinea –
not a colourful
species, but
intelligent and
vivacious.

A Dusky Lory
(Pseudeos fuscata) at
Loro Parque.

Lorikeets

One of the many sub-species of the Green-naped Lorikeet, Mitchell's *(Trichoglossus haematodus mitchellii)* is distinguished by its red breast.

Josephine's Lorikeet *(Charmosyna josefinae)* male (right) with youngster, at Loro Parque.

Male (left) and female Red-flanked Lorikeets *(Charmosyna placentis)* could be mistaken for different species.

Papaya   Unripe papaya contains the protein-splitting enzyme papain, which is highly efficient in aiding digestion. Ripe papaya contains only a small amount of papain, but is still a useful aid to digestion. It is a valuable addition to any formula used for hand-rearing chicks, but especially for chicks which are not digesting their food well. Papaya should also be given to any parrot suffering for pancreatic disorder.

Peach   This fruit is easily digested, contains vitamins and minerals and is extremely rich in carotene. However, not many parrots will eat it. For years I gave peach stones to the larger parrots in my collection, because they relish the almond-like nut in the stone, until I learned that this nut contains prussic acid which is poisonous.

Pear   Overripe fruits are always ignored – they should be juicy, not hard and certainly not mushy.

Plum   A good food if acceptable, plums contain carotene, calcium and potassium.

Pomegranate   This fruit is favoured more highly than any other by the majority of parrots. An excellent food nutritionally, it is expensive and availability is normally limited to a period of about three months. Because of its price, it is likely to be fed in moderation. Some birds would eat little else, given the opportunity, and when the season ends this could be a problem.

Prickly pear   A native of desert regions of the USA, and introduced to Mediterranean countries, this cactus fruit is not grown commercially. Where it is available locally, however, it is an excellent and inexpensive food.

Raspberry   This fruit is excellent nutritionally, but favoured by very few parrots, and usually these consume only the pips. The potassium content is high, and there are smaller amounts of calcium, magnesium, iron, carotene and the B vitamins.

Strawberry   The vitamin and mineral content of this fruit is high, but very few parrots will sample it.

G

GANG GANG COCKATOO
(*Callocephalon fimbriatum*)
The only member of its genus, this species is nearer the Black Cockatoos in appearance and behaviour, but is much smaller, being only 35 cm (13½ in). Unmistakable, it is mainly grey with lighter margins to most of the feathers; the male has a red head. Young birds can be sexed as soon as they feather.

Originating from Australia, it is rare in captivity outside that country. Of a nervous disposition and extremely susceptible to feather plucking, it should be provided with fresh-cut branches daily, and also pine cones if possible.

The diet should include plenty of small seeds (to keep the birds occupied), little or no sunflower, chicken bones, berries, such as hawthorn (eaten in the wild), and just a few mealworms.

The clutch consists of two eggs, incubated by male and female for twenty-five days. The young spend only six or seven weeks in the nest.

Geoffroyus PARROTS
This genus of parrots, from Indonesia, New Guinea and the northern tip of Australia (Cape York), is never likely to be known to aviculturists. There are records of only five birds being kept outside their country of origin, none of which survived more than a few weeks or months. One of them was recorded as eating seeds and fruit, so diet was not the problem.

There are three species, none of which appears to be rare in the wild. They are secretive birds and little is known of their natural history.

The Red-cheeked (*G. geoffroyi*), which has many sub-species almost throughout the entire range of the genus, is the most beautiful. The coloration, like the bird, is very delicate. The male's head is rose-red and pale mauve – a particularly lovely combination. The plumage is otherwise green, except for reddish-brown on the wing coverts and blue under wing coverts. The female differs in having her head brown and her beak brownish-grey. Young birds have the head green, the cheeks and throat being tinged with brown. In length this bird is about 21 cm (8½ in).

Geopsittacus – see *NIGHT PARROT*

GLAUCOUS MACAW – see under *HYACINTHINE MACAW*

Glossopsitta **LORIKEETS**
The three small lorikeets in this genus are virtually unknown outside Australia.

Extremely attractive aviary birds, they differ from other lorikeets in laying larger clutches (three to five eggs) and in the shorter period the young spend in the nest, as short as forty days in the Little Lorikeet (*G. pusilla*).

This species measures only 15 cm (6 in). Mainly green, it has the face red (duller in the female) and the beak black.

The equally small Purple-crowned (*G. porphyrocephala*) is a little gem which aviculturists outside Australia would love to obtain. Friendly and inquisitive, it can be bred on the colony system. Beautifully marked, its forehead and ear coverts are yellow and orange, its crown purple and its underparts bright blue with a yellow patch on the side of the breast. The bill is black.

The Musk Lorikeet (*G. concinna*) is currently kept in two or three zoos outside Australia. Measuring 23 cm (9 in), it has the forehead and a large patch behind the eye red, a patch of golden-brown on the mantle, and yellow on the side of the breast. This species requires a varied diet which includes plenty of seed.

GRASS PARRAKEETS
(*Neophema*)
Small and immensely popular, the Grass Parrakeets have long been favourites with beginners. Their colours are vivid, and breeding results are usually good. They originate from Australia and five of the seven species are well known in aviculture. One, the Orange-bellied (*N. chrysogaster*), is one of the most endangered birds in Australia at the present time.

Measuring 19–23 cm (8–9 in), they need only small enclosures of 1.8–2.4 m (6–8 ft) long, 76 cm (30 in) wide and 1.8 m (6 ft) high. Enclosed winter accommodation, of either a shelter or entrance to a birdroom, is recommended in colder climates, because they do not tolerate cold damp weather well. Suspended aviaries are not recommended as *Neophemas* like to walk about on the floor. Grass floors are seldom practical, but growing grass from seed in boxes and placing the boxes in the aviaries will provide these parrakeets with much enjoyment.

The diet should be as recommended for cockatiels.

Breeding usually commences at one year old, when Grass Parrakeets should be provided with a nest-box measuring 15 cm (6 in) square and about 31 cm (12 in) high. Four to six eggs, and occasionally more, form the clutch and the incubation period is about nineteen days. The female may not commence to incubate until the second or third egg has been laid. The young usually remain in the nest for twenty-eight to thirty days, sometimes less.

In an aviary longer than 1.8 m (6 ft), precautions must be taken to prevent them killing or injuring themselves by flying into the wire when they leave the nest. Consider this in advance and grow a shrub, such as honeysuckle or even convolvulus, over the end of the aviary, and place plenty of branches inside, or even tie strips of white material to the wire.

One of the most brilliantly coloured birds in existence, the male Splendid (*N. splendida*) or Scarlet-chested Parrakeet must be responsible for attracting many people to parrakeet breeding. The head, shoulders and edge of the wing are blue, the breast is scarlet and the abdomen and underside of the tail are yellow; the rest of the plumage is green. Females and young birds have the underparts entirely yellow, and the blue in the plumage is less extensive and duller. (The shade of blue is lighter than that of the female Turquoisine.)

A gentle bird, the Splendid can be kept with finches, but not with other parrakeets. In general, *Neophema* species should be

A pair of Bourke's Parrakeets.

housed as one pair per aviary and definitely not with other members of their own genus.

The male of Turquoisine (*N. pulchella*) has a dark red bar down the wing and the underparts are entirely yellow, except for an orange patch on the abdomen. Some breeders pair birds together to accentuate this feature and call the resulting young 'Orange-bellied' Turquoisines.

The female has less blue on the face than the male, lacks the red in the wing and has a breast of dull green. Immature birds are more like the female, but males often have a little red in the wing and more blue on their faces than young females.

Two species liable to cause confusion are the Elegant (*N. elegans*) and the Blue-winged (*N. chrysostoma*) Grass Parrakeets. Both have a dark blue band on the forehead, edged with lighter blue, and bright yellow lores. They are olive green above and on the upper breast, the underparts being yellow; some birds also have a touch of orange on the abdomen. The main difference lies in the wings: in the Blue-winged the wing coverts are deeper blue and this area is more extensive than in the Elegant which has most of the wing coverts green, not blue. The Elegant is a yellower shade of green, and the light blue following the dark blue on the forehead is much brighter. In the Blue-winged, the primaries are jet black in the male and brownish-black in the female. Females are duller than

males and immature birds are duller than females.

Unmistakable in its coloration, Bourke's Parrakeet (*N. bourkii*) is mainly brown above, with buff margins to the feathers, pinkish-brown below, with pink on the abdomen, and blue on the wings and on the under tail coverts. In the male the forehead is blue.

Graydidascalus brachyurus – see *SHORT-TAILED PARROT*

GREY PARROT (*Psittacus erithacus*)

The Grey Parrot, famed for its mimicry, is ever in demand. Increasingly this is being supplied by captive-bred birds, but the trade in wild-caught specimens is still substantial. This is to be deplored, because many of these are adults which are stressed by capture and by captivity, and their survival rate is not high. There should be restrictions on the export of this species, but it is, of course, a source of much-needed revenue to African countries.

Dealers advertise under different names, such as Congo Grey and Silver Grey, but there are only two sub-species. Greys do vary in the depth of grey, according to origin and sex (males normally being darker). The only sub-species known in aviculture, the Timneh (*P. e. timneh*) – not Timor, as some advertisers insist – is distinctive. It is smaller, about 29 cm (11 in) as against approximately 33 cm (13 in) for *erithacus*, has the tail dull red, not scarlet and has part of the upper mandible orange-brown.

The nominate race inhabits a wide area of western central Africa; *timneh* occurs in Liberia and a small part of the Ivory Coast, Sierra Leone and southern Guinea. The species is common in some areas, and declining in others due to the destruction of its habitat.

Although so popular, it is not necessarily an easy subject in captivity, being very easily stressed (see *STRESS* and *FEATHER PLUCKING*). Many imported birds take years to be persuaded to accept any food but sunflower seed. There is also a high risk of disease in imported birds (even although they have been quarantined for the required period). A captive-bred bird is recommended; it will cost more, but this is negligible in terms of a companion for life. The potential life-span of large parrots, such as Greys and Amazons, is sixty years, and possibly more.

Like any other parrot, in order to tame them and teach them to talk, Greys must be acquired when young, that is, while the eye is still grey or greyish-yellow (not clear yellow as in birds of one year and more). Their temperament varies greatly, but most Greys are only really friendly towards their owner or a few people whom they know well. They may exhibit a marked dislike of men or women (not invariably related to their own sex) and many will allow only one person to handle them. Generally they are not to be trusted with people they do not know, and although they turn their heads invitingly to be scratched, in many cases this is because they are awaiting the opportunity for a sly bite!

The diet should be as recommended for Amazons, but Greys do not so readily accept a wide variety of foods, unless very tame.

Compatibility is of great importance in breeding Greys. Many pairs never attempt to breed, or possibly consist of two males or two females, although the owner is convinced by their behaviour that they are a true pair. Feather or surgical sexing is advisable unless a Grey has actually laid or fertilised eggs.

The clutch usually consists of three or four eggs and the incubation period is twenty-eight to thirty days. The young spend about twelve weeks in the nest.

GRIT

Do parrots need grit? The answer is that some do and some do not. There are many different factors to take into account. In the wild, seed-eating birds of many species – not only parrots – swallow pieces of grit, shell or small stones. These end up in the gizzard (proventriculus) into which food passes after it has left the crop. The gizzard is a muscular organ in which the food is ground up before the nutrients are assimilated into the body. This is achieved by the food being rubbed against grit or other small hard items. If such items are not present, hard items of food may leave the bird's body undigested. (Note, however, that undigested particles of food in the faeces may have other causes, such as malfunction of the pancreas.)

To assess whether your birds need grit, take into consideration the following factors:

1 Diet – birds such as lories and Hanging Parrots, whose food consists almost entirely of soft items, do not need grit; indeed, the gizzard is poorly developed.

2 Birds kept in outdoor aviaries may be satisfying their need for small hard particles in the gizzard by swallowing pieces of stones from the floor, by gnawing the wall and, I suspect, by swallowing small pieces of wood gnawed from perches or branches. I know of a pair of Hyacinthine Macaws, kept at liberty, which consumed large amounts of limestones, especially while rearing a chick. Birds kept in cages have no access to such items and should be offered grit at least once a month, although it may be ignored most or even all of the time.

3 Certain species seem to have a greater need for grit than others; for example, most cockatiels and budgerigars consume it with great enthusiasm. It may be that ground-feeding species, whose diet usually consists of a greater proportion of seed than that of tree-dwelling parrots, need most. A ground-feeding Australian cockatoo, well known for its habit of picking up grit from the roads, is the Galah or Roseate. Many birds, probably mainly

young ones, are killed by vehicles as a result.

Different types and sizes of grit are available, prepared specially for cage birds. For example, one type consists mainly of crushed oystershells, perhaps with the addition of charcoal, and another type is known as mineral grit and contains various particles which provide calcium, iodine, lime, etc. As most seed diets are deficient in minerals, grit can play an important role in supplementing the diet. It should be provided in small containers which are emptied and refilled regularly, because some birds may take certain particles only and thus, though the container is half full, no more of its contents will be taken.

Grit should be limited for sick birds and those which have formerly been deprived of it and might take too much. We know that some birds in captivity feed grit to their chicks, as this has been found in the gizzard. Should grit be given to chicks being hand-reared? Much depends on the species and circumstances, and every breeder has to make up his or her own mind on this point.

One valuable function of grit is that it can break down any foreign body of reasonable size that reaches the gizzard. This was demonstrated to me in a seven-and-a-half-week-old macaw chick which I was hand-rearing. When it and its sibling were small, I was in the habit of using a plastic spoon to feed them, which is perfectly acceptable for young chicks. I retained the habit too long and one day a predictable accident occurred. The spoon broke in the chick's mouth and it swallowed a piece which was probably about 1 cm square, but of a jagged shape.

Not only was this chick especially dear to me, it also happened to be a Blue-throated or Caninde Macaw (*Ara glaucogularis*). I was aghast at my stupidity. However, the piece of plastic never appeared in the faeces and I felt there was a good chance it would stay in the gizzard. I therefore fed the young macaw a little grit once a week and he suffered no ill effects.

There is a case on record of a macaw in California, which swallowed pieces of wire off its cage. An X-ray showed that the wire was in the bird's gizzard. There was no internal bleeding so the specialist avian vet, who dealt with the case, decided not to operate. Further X-rays over a period of several months indicated that the pieces of wire were gradually becoming smaller, until they dissolved completely.

GROUND PARROT (*Pezoporus wallicus*)

The single member of this genus, also known as the Swamp Parrot, is most closely related to the Night Parrot. Its plumage is green, mottled with black and yellow, but the much longer tail and narrow red frontal band distinguish it. In length it is about 30 cm (12 in).

It is found in coastal regions of south-western and south-eastern Australia, and also in Tasmania. It lives in heath where there is thick cover and suitable food plants. It feeds on the seeds of grasses, such as buttongrass, moving around quickly, and pulling down plant stems to bring the seeding heads near to the ground. Sometimes these birds scratch in the soil with both feet, then probe with their bills, for other items of food, perhaps germinating seeds. They have long legs and run quickly, without the waddling gait of most parrots.

This species lays three or four eggs. The nest is a cup-shaped structure, perhaps at the base of a tussock of buttongrass. Chicks have dense, dark grey down and pink bills.

This species has been kept in

The Ground Parrot lives in grassy heaths and its mottled green plumage is good camouflage. Its long legs are well adapted to a terrestrial life.

captivity only rarely in Australia, but not elsewhere. The diet consists of sunflower and canary seed and millet, and greenfood, such as lucerne and milk thistle. One keeper of the Ground Parrot described it as an uninteresting aviary bird because it was mainly nocturnal, even bathing in the middle of the night.

GUAIABERO
The Guaiabero (*Bolbospittacus lunulatus*), a small, stocky parrot of 15 cm (6 in), is the only member of its genus. The tail is very short and rounded. Its throat and cheeks are blue. In the male, the area surrounding the eyes and the nuchal collar are also blue. Both sexes are otherwise green, with a yellow patch on the underside of the secondary wing feathers. The beak is bluish-grey and the iris of the eye is dark brown. The Guaiabero originates in the Philippines.

Although common in the wild, this species is virtually unknown in aviculture because it is very difficult to establish in captivity. In 1987, importers in Europe received this species for the first time. A Danish importer, who received ten birds in good condition, had no problems in persuading them to eat. They did not take seed, but consumed figs, apple, orange, carrots, berries and rose hips with relish. Regrettably, they survived only a very short time, of between one and three weeks. It appeared that they had died not of disease, but of malnutrition.

In the wild they are known to feed on berries and fruits, especially guavas (from which their name is derived), and so the fruits offered to captive birds must be deficient in some vital nutrient. San Diego Zoo kept two alive, for six and eight months, in 1962. The Swiss aviculturist Dr R. Burkard also kept this species for a short while. His fed on potato, sweet potato and fruit. They were described as quiet and slow moving, but liable to fly off suddenly and injure themselves if startled.

Those received in Denmark were described as being very beautiful, of the same shade of green as male Eclectus Parrots and the same size as *Psittaculirostris* Fig Parrots. Their behaviour is said to be not unlike that of the latter.

HABITAT
Parrots are essentially birds of the tropics, where they occur in many different types of habitat. However, not all of them originate from hot or warm climates. There are a considerable number of mountain species which spend most of their lives at high altitudes, even in cloud forest. Chicks of many parrot species have thick down, to keep them warm when nights are cold, or days are cool.

The species with the most southerly distribution is the Austral Conure (*Enicognathus f. ferrugineus*) from the coldest part of South America – Tierra del Fuego, where the climate is bleak and hostile. In New Zeland, the Kea (*Nestor notabilis*) is found in the Alps where it plays in the snow!

Even species which inhabit Caribbean islands can spend most of their days in a cool temperature; for example, the St Vincent Parrot (*Amazona guildingii*) lives only in the mountains where it has been pushed to higher altitudes by human encroachment (once it occurred throughout the island). Here, cloud cover results in the temperature being quite chilly for most of the day.

Tropical rainforest, however, is the type of habitat in which species and individual parrots are most plentiful. The climate is hot, varies little throughout the year and produces an abundance of food at all times. Some species are found in a wide variety of habitats throughout their range, whereas others have very specialised requirements. For example, the numerous and widely distributed Orange-winged Amazon is found in rainforest, mangrove forest, savannah forest, timbered coastal sand ridges and cacao plantations.

In contrast, the Tucuman Amazon (*A. tucumana*), from Bolivia and Argentina, is a bird of forests of alder (*Alnus jorullensis*). The closely related Pretre's Amazon (*A. pretrei*), from south-east Brazil and north-east Argentina, is found only in

Araucaria forest, and the seeds of this tree are its most favoured food.

Some species are nomadic, moving about according to the food supply. One of the most nomadic species of northern Australia, for example, is the cockatiel (*Nymphicus hollandicus*). These birds' movements are most marked during dry seasons when they may suddenly appear in areas where they have not been seen for years.

Some species have highly specialised habitats. Among the Grass Parrakeets (*Neophemas*), the Rock Parrakeet (*N. petrophila*) is found only among coastal sand dunes and offshore rocky islets of southern Australia. The least specialised member of the genus is the Blue-winged Parrakeet (*N. chrysostoma*) from south-eastern Australia and Tasmania. It, too, occurs in coastal sand dunes and also in saltbush plains, forest, sparsely timbered grasslands and acacia scrublands.

In many parts of Australia parrots and man live in close, but not happy, association. Parrots are considered to be pests which destroy crops, especially grain. Cockatoos destroy more than crops; they even descend on houses and vandalise the wooden roofs. They are extremely unpopular, and shooting and poisoning are accepted methods of exterminating them. Despite this parrots can be seen in city parks and gardens.

In many parts of the tropics, however, parrots live quite happily in close association with man. In plenty of South American towns, parrots are as numerous as people in the main squares. In Leticia, Colombia, I saw a huge flock of Canary-winged Parrakeets leave their roost in such a location at first light, and in São Paulo, in a small park surrounded by skyscrapers, another *Brotogeris* parrakeet, the All-green (*B. tirica*) can be observed.

I well remember looking out of the window of a hotel in the Andes of Colombia, to see a tiny Spectacled Parrotlet (*Forpus conspicillatus*) perched on a stark lamp standard. It seemed so incongruous.

In India, the Ringneck Parrakeet (*Psittacula krameri*) is very common in the vicinity of the larger cities, such as New Delhi, and is seen in gardens and orchards.

In short, parrots will be found in almost any location as long as it provides food and nest sites.

HANDLING

All species of parrots, even the small ones, can bite very hard, and most will not hesitate to do so when handled. When catching them, the aim is to immobilise the mandibles by placing a thumb and forefinger on either side of the beak. It is often difficult to maintain this grip, as the large species are very strong, and thus it is best to transfer the bird to a towel at once, keeping the mandibles closed.

It is much easier to control a bird held within a towel and to catch one by putting a towel over its head, yet retaining one's grip on its beak. A proper catching net should be used to remove birds from an aviary. Gloves are not

Only young parrots such as the Leadbeater's Cockatoos shown here can be handled in such a casual manner.

recommended for catching and handling; they frighten parrots and make it difficult for the handler to hold the bird efficiently.

HAND-REARING

Rearing parrot chicks by hand is very time-consuming and limits one's other activities; abandoned chicks are often better placed with foster parents. However, chicks are often hand-reared because the tame young which result are in great demand as pets. A brooder is essential in a cool climate. In a warm climate a heat pad may suffice.

A spoon with the sides bent inwards is the best implement for feeding. The food must be warm and fairly runny; if unsure of the correct consistency, it is better to add more water than give food which is too thick. The frequency of feeds will vary according to the size and crop capacity of the chick (those that have been fed by their parents, or other birds, usually have a larger capacity). The crop should never be filled to the maximum, even although this means feeding more often.

Newly hatched chicks will need to be fed every hour and a half on very liquid food, and those approaching weaning should be fed every three or four hours on thicker food. Feeds should be given between about 6.30 a.m. and 11 p.m., if possible.

Hand-rearing is a very complex subject which cannot be covered in a few paragraphs. Many, many different foods are used, according to the species and the inclination of the feeder. These and other aspects are covered fully in *Hand-rearing Parrots* by Rosemary Low, published by Blandford Press.

Foods commonly used consist of a mixture of dry baby cereal (at least 15% protein) and some fruit, either fresh, such as papaya or apple, or tinned baby meals, adding wheat germ cereal and sunflower seed kernels (available from health food stores) at about ten days. These items should be mixed with water in a blender, then cooked or heated well. Additives such as calcium (or vitamins in exceptional cases – there should be enough in the food) should be added to the spoon as the food is given, as heating destroys their value in most cases.

A spoon with the sides bent inwards is the best instrument for hand-feeding chicks, such as this Iris Lorikeet (*Trichoglossus iris*).

Weaning should be a very gradual process and can take as long as eight months to accomplish in large species such as macaws, although most parrots will be weaned by four to five months, or sooner in the small species. Foods enjoyed by chicks being weaned include corn on the cob, soaked sunflower seed, bread, millet spray, apple and papaya.

HANGING PARROTS (*Loriculus*)

Hanging Parrots could be described as the tiny gems of the parrot family. Their feeding and care demand a little more time than that of most parrots, but the pleasure provided by their beauty, diminutiveness and interesting behaviour is worth the extra effort.

The name is derived from the fact that these birds normally roost hanging upside down, from the wire roof of an aviary or from a perch. However, a breeder of several species of *Loriculus* told me that some female Philippine Hanging Parrots in his collection do not roost in this way, and that neither do birds which are sick.

These tiny birds, measuring 11–12 cm (4½–5 in), are mainly green, with the beak red, orange or blue and contrasting colours on the throat and/or crown and on the upper tail coverts. Aviculturally, they should be regarded more like softbills than parrots, and are seen at their best in a planted aviary, with softbills or finches.

Hanging Parrots can be kept and bred on the colony system, but because they need livefood when rearing young, and the competition for this food is too great in a mixed aviary, the best breeding results will be achieved when each pair have an enclosure to themselves.

There is a subtle or marked degree of sexual dimorphism,

according to the species, which originate in Asia, Indonesia and New Guinea.

The most commonly imported species is the Vernal (*L. vernalis*) which has a wide area of distribution, including India, Burma, Assam, Thailand, the Malay Peninsula, Cambodia, Laos and Vietnam. A common species, it feeds on fruits, berries, small seeds and nectar. It is light green, with a pale blue patch on the throat and a red rump and tail coverts. The only sexual distinction is the eye colour, the iris being white in the male and brown in the female.

In my opinion, the most beautiful species – indeed, one of the most exquisite of all small parrots – is the Blue-crowned (*L. galgulus*). Its brilliant colours are unrivalled, as is the texture of its feathers, and the almost luminous quality of the red in the plumage. The tiny black beak adds to its beauty: the overall effect is one of neatness found in few other psittacines.

Both sexes have a blue patch on the crown and a triangular patch of tawny gold on the mantle, which are duller in the female. Rump and upper tail coverts, perhaps the most beautiful feature of the species, are scarlet, and also the throat in the male.

A Danish breeder told me that they can be sexed at about six months, when the blue on the male's head starts to appear. At this stage an immature male can be distinguished from an adult female by his brighter scarlet rump. The red on the throat is the last colour to appear. By the age of one year, the male is in full adult plumage.

Also available is the Philippine Hanging Parrot (*L. philippensis*). This is the largest Hanging Parrot, of which there are eleven sub-species. In the nominate race, the forehead and crown are red, followed by a dusky yellow patch and the nape is decorated with a golden-orange band. The male has a large red patch on the throat, and the female has pale blue lores. Immature birds have very little red on the forehead.

The other six species are very rare in captivity. One which was virtually unknown until 1984 is the Celebes or Red-crowned (*L. stigmatus*) from the islands of the Celebes in Indonesia. A vivid shade of green, the male's plumage is set off by a scarlet forehead, crown, throat, rump and tail coverts. The beak is black and the iris pale yellow. The female is all green, with the iris brown. Immature birds are mainly green, slightly darker above, with a tiny orange spot on the throat. The rump is red and the tail, as in the adults, is light blue on the underside.

Because their diet consists partly of fruit, which is flicked in all directions, it would be advisable to keep these birds indoors only in a cage made specially for them. It should be constructed of a material, such as melamine, which is easy to clean, and perhaps have the front made of glass. Ease of cleaning should also be borne in mind in a small aviary. In a large enclosure their feeding habits are not a problem.

A wide variety of foods should be offered, with unlimited fruit being given to newly imported birds, and also boiled sweetened rice, which many are offered in the country of export. When half an apple is provided, only the thin shell of the skin will be left. All the usual fruits, nectar, or sponge cake and nectar, small seeds such as canary and soaked or sprouted sunflower (small), spray millet and pure fruit juices will be taken. One breeder provides his Hanging Parrots with yoghurt blended with sugar, pollen meal with glucose, and peas, plus various fruits.

Protein, preferably of animal origin, is essential when young are being reared. Ants' eggs and mealworms, dusted with a multivitamin and mineral preparation, are the best forms of livefood: maggots introduce a risk of botulism unless cleaned for several days in bran or sand.

The nest-box provided for these birds should have a small base, about 11 cm (4½ in) square, but should be high enough to allow them to line it with a deep layer of leaves. These are necessary to keep the nest dry during the rearing period. Females will carry leaves into the nest in the feathers of their breast or rump. At Loro Parque, where only pine branches are provided, a female Philippine lined her nest with small pieces of pine.

Courtship behaviour is

fascinating to observe. I am compelled to stop and watch if I pass the Blue-crowns' aviary when the male is displaying. It is a wonderful sight: the red feathers of the throat seem to be inflated. Most extraordinary of all is the manner in which the male feeds the female. A globule of food protrudes from his beak, almost like a child blowing bubble gum, and is sucked in by the female. Hanging Parrots lay three, and occasionally four, eggs, which are incubated by the female for twenty days. The young spend just under five weeks in the nest.

These small birds should not be expected to tolerate low temperatures. A heated shelter or indoor accommodation should be provided in the winter.

HATCHING FAILURE

There are many reasons why eggs fail to hatch and it is usually very difficult to determine which one is responsible. Death of the embryo during any stage of incubation could be due to dirty conditions in the nest, resulting in bacteria entering the egg, or to a dietary deficiency. If the embryo is deficient in some vital element, it will die. This is why a mineral and vitamin additive is recommended for females prior to laying. It should be added to a popular item of food with which it will easily combine, such as bread and milk, not given in the drinking water where it will affect the taste more noticeably, possibly resulting in the bird not drinking.

Death of the embryo due to insufficient humidity is rarer than was formerly believed. In fact, many parrot eggs which are artificially incubated, require little or no water during incubation, until the chick pips the shell, when humidity should be greatly increased.

Excessive humidity is a common cause of embryonic death. An egg must lose about 16% of its weight through evaporation during incubation; if the environment is too wet, this is impossible and the embryo dies. Weight loss is also related to the pore structure of the eggshell; eggs with very porous shells seldom hatch unless they are weighed daily and the humidity within the incubator controlled to maintain the correct weight loss.

Thin-shelled eggs usually fail to hatch, either because they are unintentionally damaged by the incubating bird (who may then be blamed for egg-breaking) or because there is insufficient calcium available for the developing embryo, which draws on the calcium within the eggshell.

Dead-in-shell is the term for chicks which die in the egg, fully formed, and just prior to hatching. It is not correct to use this term for the death of the embryo at an earlier stage. One of the most common reasons is low environmental temperature, thus dead-in-shell is common in birds breeding in outdoor aviaries during the winter.

A not uncommon cause of hatching failure is that the egg membrane (the layer between the chick and the shell) is so firmly attached to the chick's head that the chick is unable to rotate within the egg, to hatch. I have removed many parrot chicks from the egg in

A Solomon Eclectus Parrot (*Eclectus roratus solomonensis*) in the final stages of hatching.

Assisted hatching.

these circumstances: they would have died unless assisted. All have grown into excellent specimens, thus the reason for hatching failure in this case is not that the chick is weak. If assistance in hatching is left too late, the chick will die because it has used up all the available oxygen and its brain suffers damage.

Incidentally, the period from pipping to hatching varies tremendously, from a few hours to as long as three days.

Eggs which fail to hatch because they are infertile cannot be distinguished from those in which the embryo dies during the first few hours of incubation. Something in the region of 25% of all embryonic deaths are believed to occur during the first three to five days of incubation.

The reasons for infertility are that mating has not occurred, or it has occurred, but one, or both, birds are not in full breeding condition. A problem with many parrots, especially Amazons, is that male and female do not simultaneously achieve breeding condition. Another cause of infertile eggs, in adult birds as well as inexperienced young ones, is that the male does not learn to copulate correctly.

HAWK-HEADED PARROT
(*Deroptyus accipitrinus accipitrinus*)
The single member of this genus is one of the most distinctive of parrots. It is recognised by its erectile head feathers of maroon margined with blue, a colour scheme which is repeated on the underparts. The head feathers are brown, prominently shaft-streaked with buff. The feathers of the forehead are whitish in the nominate race and dusky brown in the sub-species *fuscifrons*. The upperparts are green. Immature birds have some green on the head and the blue margins to the feathers are more greenish.

In length it is about 31 cm (12 in). Plumage is alike in male and female.

This species comes from the Amazon basin (the Guianas, Brazil, Colombia and Peru), where it occurs in small groups. Occasionally imported, it has never been common in aviculture and breeding successes are not frequent. Compatibility can be a

The Hawk-headed Parrot (*Deroptyus accipitrinus accipitrinus*) is most distinctive in plumage and behaviour.

problem, as adult birds can be extremely aggressive (towards humans as well as other Hawk-heads). When two are introduced, there should be two feeding points in the aviary to ensure that one bird is not kept away from the food by the other, dominant one.

The threat display of the Hawk-headed Parrot is spectacular: the maroon and blue head feathers are erected to form a ruff and the bird sways from side to side in a menacing manner, emitting a whining sound. This would undoubtedly be effective in frightening off enemies.

Hawk-heads require a diet containing much fresh fruit, in addition to seeds such as sunflower, canary, millet, buckwheat, spray millet and the usual vegetables and berries, especially hawthorn which are greatly relished. Bread and milk can also be offered, especially when the birds are breeding.

This is a nervous parrot which is not easy to breed. If successful, two or three eggs are laid and incubated by the female for about twenty-six days. The young leave the nest after about nine weeks. Hand-reared young are delightful, as tame Hawk-heads can be endearingly affectionate.

It should be noted that this species can be extremely noisy.

A nest-box should always be available for roosting.

HYACINTHINE MACAW
(*Anodorhynchus hyacinthinus*)

Named for its colour of hyacinth blue, this is the largest of all parrots, and also one of the most magnificent. Its appearance evokes more gasps of admiration and surprise in those seeing it for the first time, than almost any other parrot. Its sheer size, and that of its beak, are awe-inspiring.

In length it is about 92 cm (36 in), and it weighs about 1,250–1,400 g (42½–47½ oz). The eyes and lower mandible are surrounded by bright yellow skin.

Lear's Macaw (*A. leari*) has a similar coloration, but is smaller, being only about 75 cm (30 in).

The mysterious Glaucous Macaw (*A. glaucus*) is said to be extinct, not having been recorded in the wild since the nineteenth century. It resembled the Lear's, except for the slightly different shade of its plumage.

The Hyacinthine originates from the interior of Brazil, south of the Amazon, and also from extreme eastern Bolivia and north-eastern Paraguay. It is declining because of the volume of trade and the disturbance of its habitat, much of which has been settled in recent years. The origin of Lear's Macaw was discovered as recently as 1978, in north-eastern Bahia in Brazil. Only one population is known to exist, which consists of about 100 birds and possibly fewer.

A tame Hyacinthine Macaw is remarkably docile. It could sever a finger as easily as a person breaking a match, yet it is gentle and affectionate, with a dog-like devotion to its human friends. In the USA hand-reared birds are in demand as pets – among those wealthy enough to be able to afford one. Few parrots command a higher price. Equally, few people can afford the time or the accommodation needed for such a demanding and beautiful creature.

It is to be hoped that many Hyacinthines, obtained as pets, are given the opportunity to breed when mature, or, certainly in the USA, the future of the species in aviculture will not be secure.

An increase of animal protein (cooked meat, hard-boiled egg, canned dog food) may encourage these birds to breed. The normal diet should include plenty of large nuts (especially walnuts and Brazil nuts) and sunflower seed. Newly imported birds may have to be offered coconut if they refuse all other foods. The diet should also contain corn on the cob, dog biscuits, or those made for other animals, such as ZuPreem (Zu/Preem, Hill's Division Riviana Foods Inc, POB 148, Topeka, Ks 66601, USA), plenty of fruit, boiled maize, peas, boiled beans and sprouted wheat and/or oats. One pair consumed large amounts of green hazel nuts after their chick was six weeks old.

Captive-bred females will lay as early as four or five years old. Nest sites used in captivity have included a steel drum (227-litre/50-gal), a whisky barrel mounted on its side, and strong wooden nest-boxes. The two eggs are incubated by the female for twenty-eight or twenty-nine days. The young resemble the adults, except for a paler yellow skin and slightly duller plumage. When rearing young, Hyacinthines need plenty of limestone or large grit.

This species is being bred in an increasing number of American and European collections. The young are very aware, intelligent and lovable. Their enormous feet at the fledgling stage lend them an air of ungainly charm!

Lear's Macaw is extremely rare

The Hyacinthine Macaw (*Anodorhynchus hyacinthinus*) has the most massive bill of any parrot; its strength is enormous.

in captivity; only about twelve birds are known outside Brazil. These include only one breeding pair, at Busch Gardens, Tampa, Florida. The male of this pair had been on exhibit at Parrot Jungle in Miami for twenty-seven years before being sent to Tampa in 1982. Within two months of their introduction, the female laid three eggs which were infertile. Two young from this pair survive (off-exhibit) at Busch gardens.

HYGIENE
Hygiene is a vitally important part of good management. Many birdkeepers do not realise how important it is until a bird dies as a result of a bacterial disease, or, worse, an outbreak occurs which kills a number of birds. Disease can be introduced to the occupants of an outdoor aviary by wild birds whose faeces fall into the enclosure.

However, when the occupants' faeces are allowed to accumulate, and mould grows on them and on discarded food, there is a danger of a fungus disease being contracted. Cages contaminated by the droppings of mice (or wild birds) could be a source of pseudotuberculosis, for example, thus regular cleaning and disinfection are necessary. A veterinarian or pet store should be able to recommend a suitable disinfectant for outdoor aviaries and birdrooms.

Cleanliness must also extend to food and water pots, blocks used for chopping food, containers for seed and other foods. Perches must be changed or washed regularly (mites will live in cracks and in the space between the end of the perch and the side of the aviary). Nest-boxes must also be cleaned and disinfected, as they can be a prime source of bacteria and mites.

Food and water pots must be cleaned daily.

I

ILLNESS
The symptoms of ill health to watch for are inactivity and sleepiness, frequent blinking of the eyes, dull eyes, ruffled feathers and an impression that the bird feels cold, discharge from the eyes and/or nostrils, soiled vent feathers and general weakness. Most sick birds rest with two feet on the perch (instead of one foot as is normal in adult birds), while the head is tucked into the feathers of the back.

Other symptoms are lack of appetite (if much food remains in the dish when normally it is empty, this is an immediate cause for concern) and faeces which differ from normal in colour and consistency – remember, however, that certain items of food can also produce this effect.

The priorities for a sick bird are warmth (see *INFRA-RED LAMP*), isolation, to prevent the spread of disease and also to ensure that the bird is undisturbed, veterinary attention and suitable food. A sick bird may have to be tempted to eat by offering favourite items, or it may require a soft food, such as bread and milk, even although it does not normally take this. If it refuses food it may have to be force-fed (see *FORCE-FEEDING*).

See also *STRESS, WINTER CARE* and *ANTIBIOTICS*.

INCUBATION
The embryo within an egg can develop only if it is maintained at the correct temperature; in parrots this is approximately 37°C (99°F). Incubation is the process of applying heat to the egg. Heat is applied via the brood patch, an area on the abdomen of the bird. When it lowers itself onto the eggs, it ruffles the feathers in that area to expose the patch. In most parrots, only the female incubates; in others, notably cockatoos (and also some *Vini* and *Charmosyna* lories), both sexes share incubation duties.

The incubation period in parrots varies from fourteen to twenty-nine days under optimum conditions, depending upon the species. That is, in cold weather, a species with a normal incubation period of, say, twenty-three days, could have that period prolonged by three or even four days. Likewise, in hot weather, the incubation period could be shortened by one or two days. (Such information can be obtained only by the study of birds in captivity.)

By far the shortest incubation period of any parrot is that of the Lesser Vasa (*Coracopsis nigra*) – only fourteen days. It is possible that the same applies to the Greater Vasa (*C. vasa*), but this species has yet to be bred in captivity and nothing is known about it in the wild. In many respects, the *Coracopsis* species are aberrant; they are not truly representative members of the parrot family, in my opinion.

The next shortest incubation periods are those recorded in Australian parrakeets: that for the budgerigar is eighteen days, for others it is usually nineteen days.

The longest incubation period, of about twenty-nine days, is found in some cockatoos and in the Hyacinthine Macaw. Here, perhaps, I may be permitted to correct Joseph Forshaw who, in his excellent book *Parrots of the World*, states: 'Duration of incubation varies roughly in proportion to the size of the bird; for small parrots it is from seventeen to twenty-three days, but for the large macaws it can be up to five weeks.'

Many lories have an incubation period of twenty-five days, from the smallest *Vini* to the largest *Lorius* (size range 17–31 cm/6½–12 in) although in most *Trichoglossus*, which are midway in size, the incubation period is twenty-three days. There are many other examples to denote that the size theory is untrue.

It must be remembered that not all parrots commence to incubate when the first egg is laid, although the female may be in the nest from this time. Also, unless the eggs are marked as laid, and all the eggs in the clutch hatch, it may be difficult to obtain accurate records of incubation periods. In fact, the only way is to place a newly laid egg in an incubator.

The incubation period is actually defined as the length of time from the laying of the last egg in the clutch to the hatching of that egg, assuming that there are no interruptions, other than the normal few minutes' absence from the nest by the incubating bird.

During the incubation period, most eggs lose about 16% of their weight, because of water loss from the contents through the porous shell. The eggshell porosity of species which nest at high altitudes is reduced, to compensate for the changes that would result in embryonic respiratory gas exchange and water loss from the egg, as a consequence of low barometric pressure. Breeders who use an incubator must, therefore, bear in mind that humidity requirements within the incubator may vary according to the species.

INCUBATORS

The number of models available to aviculturists has increased greatly in recent years. It may therefore be difficult to make a choice. The following guidelines are suggested:

1 Choose a model made by a well-established company, which has been in use for some years. One sees various makes come and go, especially at the low-price end of the range. Some appear to have been produced without sufficient testing.

2 Choose a small model. Large incubators are ideal for commercial poultry breeders, but they operate best when full – and the capacity will be a thousand eggs or more. Few private breeders will require an incubator with a capacity of more than thirty or forty eggs. In any case, it is more practical to use several small incubators, because each one can be kept at a different humidity, thereby giving better control for the requirements of individual eggs.

3 Choose an incubator which is easy to keep clean.

4 Choose one with the heat source in the centre. Failing this, place the thermometer as near the eggs as possible, or an accurate temperature reading will not be obtained.

5 Choose a forced-air model. Few still-air incubators are available these days, because the temperature fluctuations are unacceptable in such models. If

one is used, the temperature (see *INCUBATION*) will need to be 2 or 3° F higher than that recommended for forced-air machines

My own recommendation for the small breeder would be a Marsh Farms Turn-X or the larger Roll-X. Most incubators have automatic turning devices. These are useful for people who are unable to turn eggs at frequent intervals (at least four times a day is recommended). However, those who can, may prefer to turn the eggs by hand (as I do) as some models may not treat the eggs as gently as one would wish.

Do not keep an incubator in a room which is subject to temperature fluctuations, such as a kitchen. Avoid situations where the sun could strike the incubator, thus increasing the temperature. Keep the incubator out of reach of children and animals. Ensure that an accurate thermometer is used.

This virtually unbreakable ceramic infra-red lamp, which emits heat only, is ideal for use with sick birds.

A digital thermometer is recommended for brooder and incubator: it is very quick to register any change in temperature and also easy to read.

Those fitted to many incubators are either inaccurate or difficult to read, or both. A digital thermometer is recommended (see *BROODERS*).

Ensure that the incubator is sterilised or fumigated between hatches. Fumigation can be carried out as follows: place a pinch of crystals of potassium permanganate in a small container inside the incubator. Then add a teaspoonful of formaldehyde (37% solution) to the crystals. Close the lid and leave the room quickly, because a very powerful and unpleasant gas is given off. Leave alone for twenty-four hours.

INFRA-RED LAMP

The first step to take when a bird is unwell – or even just suffering from shock (unless the temperature is already in the region of 30°C [86°F]) – is to place it in warm surroundings. This should not be by a radiator or in an airing cupboard, as is sometimes recommended, but in a concentrated source of heat from which the bird can move away if it desires. The best source is undoubtedly an infra-red lamp. Hospital cages for parrots are seldom practical; in any case their even temperature does not allow the occupant to escape excessive heat, and also the atmosphere is extremely dry.

There are various types of infra-red lamps, such as the short-wave emitters made of glass. These are useful, but not the best. The bright glare of the lamp is not restful for a sick bird, the glass is vulnerable to explosion and breakage (especially as a result of being splashed by water) and some of the energy is dissipated as light. Possibly, also, the vitamin content of the food in the cage is destroyed.

The type of infra-red lamp which I have used for years, and which I would never be without, is the dull emitter (no light) with a ceramic element. It is virtually unbreakable, unaffected by water splashes and has an extremely long life (the bright emitter does not). The low filament temperature eliminates fire risk. (In the UK this type of lamp can be obtained from Infrared International Ltd, 52 St Francis Road, Salisbury, Wilts SP1 3QZ.)

K

KAKA (*Nestor meridionalis*)

This bird originates in New Zealand. It shows sexual dimorphism, in that the bill is usually longer and more curved in the male. In length it is about 45 cm (18 in). It is extremely rare in captivity.

The Kaka is a large and unusually coloured bird, being mainly greenish-brown with the rump and upper and under tail coverts crimson barred with dark brown. The ear coverts are orange-yellow, and the under wing coverts and the underside of the flight feathers are scarlet. In immature birds the base of the lower mandible is yellow.

Kakas were kept at London Zoo as long ago as 1863, but none had been seen outside New Zealand in this century until Stuttgart Zoo, in West Germany, received a pair in 1986. These were bred in Auckland Zoo, which has been consistently successful in rearing Kakas since 1981.

The three or four eggs are incubated for twenty-eight days. Newly hatched chicks are covered in white down, and spend nine or ten weeks in the nest.

In captivity Kakas feed on seeds, fruits and vegetables, and also on nectar and brown bread. Nectar is an important part of their diet in the wild. When feeding on pollen, some pollen adheres to their heads, resulting in cross-pollination of flax and other plants. Kakas also consume harmful insects and grubs and therefore play an important role in the ecology of the New Zealand forests. With their long, hooked beaks they dig out large grubs, such as those of the corn beetle, which are 10–13 cm (4–5 in) in length.

Unfortunately, Kakas have declined appreciably in the wild, because of deforestation.

KAKAPO (*Strigops habroptilus*)

The Kakapo is one of the most interesting birds in existence, and, sadly, it is also one of the most endangered. It has a number of features of appearance and behaviour which make it unique among parrots – even unique among birds. The heaviest parrot (1–3.4 kg/2–7½ lb – males being heavier than females), it is large, over 60 cm (2 ft) in length, with a short tail. The soft plumage is barred and streaked throughout with brown and yellow, being mainly green above and greenish-yellow below. Its normal stance is near-horizontal.

Flightless and mainly nocturnal, it is also a *lek* species, the only lek parrot and the only flightless lek bird. Lek is a mating system in which males congregate and perform displays on traditionally established grounds. The male has an inflatable thoracic air sac with which it produces a booming call, the aim of which is to attract a female. (As many as 1,000 booms per hour have been recorded.) Booming does not occur every year, but only when breeding attempts are made – probably only when food is sufficiently abundant.

Alas, the number of females left in existence is so small that, despite the heroic efforts of the New Zealand Wildlife Service, the species is on the very brink of extinction. It evolved in the absence of mammalian predators and, being flightless and nesting on the ground, it is not equipped to cope with them.

Historically, the Kakapo's biggest enemy was man. At one time Kakapo was the principal food of the Maoris. They also hunted it relentlessly for its highly prized skins (cloaks were made from the feathers). When the European settlers arrived, this magnificent parrot was exterminated in most areas – by intentional killing and through the introduction of rats, stoats, cats and dogs.

Today, the population numbers in the region of forty individuals. Since the late 1970s intensive efforts have been made to protect the survivors of one of the most fascinating species ever to have evolved.

KAKARIKIS (*Cyanoramphus*)

Kakarikis are perhaps the most active parrots in existence and make delightful aviary birds. Found only in New Zealand and its offshore islands, there are two species, the Red-fronted (*C.

novaezelandiae), which measures about 28 cm (11 in), and the Yellow-fronted (*C. auriceps*) which is about 25 cm (10 in) long. The latter also has a red forehead, but is immediately identified by the yellow area behind the red. Immature birds have the iris brown (red in adults) and, in the Red-fronted, less red on the head.

Kakarikis are fearless, inquisitive in the extreme (an exit will soon be made from the aviary if a hole develops) and usually exceptionally prolific. They mature earlier than any other parrot of comparable size and have been known to produce young at only five months old. They need a fairly large nest, approximately 23–25 cm (9–10 in) square and 31 cm (12 in) high, to accommodate what may be a very large family.

As many as ten or eleven chicks have been hatched in one clutch. However, the usual clutch is five to nine eggs, and the incubation period is about nineteen days. The young spend five to six weeks in the nest. During this period a rearing food must be provided in addition to the usual seeds, fruits and vegetables. Mealworms will be enjoyed during this time. A very wide range of foods will be eaten, especially greenfoods of all kinds, a fresh turf of grass, and the berries of hawthorn and elder.

Kakarikis spend a lot of time on the ground, scratching and picking up items of food: they are therefore very susceptible to worms and must be wormed at least twice a year. Long-legged birds, they can run very fast (also up and down welded mesh), without the waddling gait of most parrots which have short legs.

They can be unreservedly recommended to beginners (who will enjoy their prolificacy) and to more experienced breeders. Their pleasant voices will not disturb anyone and their friendly personalities always give pleasure. They are not destructive or aggressive and can even be kept with small birds such as finches, but they should not be kept with other parrots who will be annoyed by their inquisitive antics.

KEA (*Nestor notabilis*)

In its large size (48 cm/19 in), bronze-green plumage and elongated beak, the Kea is quite unlike any other parrot in aviculture. The most colourful areas of the plumage, the orange-red rump and under wing coverts, are seldom visible when the bird is perched. The bill is usually shorter and less curved in the female.

An inhabitant of the mountains of New Zealand's South Island, Keas are noted for their inquisitive and playful habits. A century ago, they had a reputation as sheep killers and a bounty was placed on their heads. Thousands were killed. However, far from becoming extinct, as some predicted, they remain fairly common to this day and are now partly protected. It would be a tragedy if this endearing and highly intelligent parrot was to become extinct.

They are fascinating aviary birds, often bounding sideways along the ground with their heads cocked upwards. Vocally, they are unlike any other parrot, and their distinctive quavering cry can be heard throughout the night as well as during the day. In the wild they nest on the ground, in crevices among rocks or tree roots; in an aviary a nest site can be made out of rocks or a horizontal nest-box placed on the ground. They will use a box at a higher level also.

Three or four eggs are laid and incubated for about twenty-nine days. The young spend about ten weeks in the nest. Animal protein, in the form of meat, young mice and mealworms, is required during the rearing period. They will eat almost anything in the way of table scraps (meat, potatoes, rice, bread) and also root vegetables, such as whole carrots and beetroot. The wider the variety of items offered, the better.

The Kea is not common in captivity outside New Zealand, being bred in comparatively few collections, and therefore it is expensive to purchase. They are endearing and amusing and anyone fortunate enough to own a pair should make every effort to persuade them to breed.

KING PARRAKEETS (*Alisterus*)

The Kings are extremely beautiful parrakeets with long, broad tails. One species comes from Australia, one from New Guinea and a third, with a distinctive sub-species, from

Indonesia. Only the Australian King is fairly common in captivity.

They need a spacious aviary, 5–6 m (16–19 ft) long to be seen at their best. However, when the young fledge in an enclosure of this length, precautions must be taken to prevent them flying at speed into the wire and killing themselves. For this reason, a mass of branches should be placed in front of the welded mesh.

They accept a varied diet of the usual seeds, pine nuts, greenfood and fruit. A rearing food, spray millet, fresh corn on the cob and extra greenfood should be offered when young are being reared. Berries of hawthorn and elder, and rose hips are also eaten.

Kings lay two to four eggs, or up to five in the Australian species. The incubation period is twenty-one days and the young remain in the nest for about eight weeks. They are not among the easiest birds to breed, yet some pairs can prove prolific. A pair of Green-winged Kings, of the sub-species *moszkowskii*, at Loro Parque hatched nine young in three nests in 1987. The second nest of three were reared by the parents, but the other chicks were removed for hand-rearing.

There was a sad sequel to this wonderful performance. When the rain came in October, it stimulated the male to nest again – but the female was not in breeding condition. He attacked her and she died from the head injuries she received. This is a problem of which owners of Kings should be constantly aware – although it is not necessarily the male who is the aggressor in the island Kings. It is often necessary to cut the flight feathers of the male when a new female is introduced, to prevent her being chased and stressed.

The Australian King (*A. scapularis*) is the largest, with a length of about 43 cm (17 in). The male is green with head and underparts scarlet, while the female's head is green and she is duller throughout, as are immature birds. A yellow mutation has been bred.

The Green-winged King (*A. chloropterus*) from New Guinea is a very striking bird. It is rare in aviculture and very expensive. Slightly smaller and more slender than the Australian King, with the

An Australian King Parrakeet (*Alisterus scapularis*), aged nineteen days.

mantle dark blue, there is a yellowish-green patch extending along the wing coverts.

The female of the nominate race can be distinguished from the Australian species by her deeper blue rump and reddish tinge to the underparts. The female of the race *moszkowskii* lacks blue on the mantle, but is otherwise as colourful as the male. In nest feather some young males have dark blue on the mantle; others do not.

Little known until the mid 1970s, the Amboina King (*A. amboinensis amboinensis*) has blue on its mantle, and green wings with blue at the bend. The tail is blue above. The shade of red on head and underparts is dark. The upper mandible is red on the upper part and black on the lower half, and the lower mandible is black (as in *chloropterus*). Not common, this species is being bred in a few collections. In one, the female ignored all nest-boxes until one was placed on the ground; there she reared a single chick.

A male Australian Crimson-winged Parrakeet *(Aprosmictus erythropterus erythropterus)*.

Parrakeets (1)

The male Barraband's *(Polytelis swainsonii)* is one of the most elegant of all the Australian parrakeets.

Above: A male Many-coloured Parrakeet *(Psephotus varius).*

Young Orange-flanked Parrakeets *(Brotogeris pyrrhopterus)* can be recognised by their dark beaks. The two young with this pair were bred at Loro Parque.

L

LEAR's MACAW – see under *HYACINTHINE MACAW*

Leptosittaca CONURE

The single member of this genus, known as Branicki's or the Golden-plumed Conure (*L. branickii*), appears to have been separated from the *Aratinga* species only because it possesses elongated yellow feathers above the ear coverts. Mainly green, it has a narrow yellow frontal band, yellow lores and a yellow line of feathers below the eye. The cere is partly feathered. The abdomen is mottled with orange. In length this bird is 35 cm (14 in).

Very little is known about this conure, which occurs in the Andes of Colombia, south-western Ecuador and central Peru. It has never been exported.

Loriculus – see *HANGING PARROTS*

LORIES

The lories and lorikeets (collectively known as lories) are a distinctive group of birds which originate from Indonesia, New Guinea, Australia and the islands of the Pacific. In the wild, the principal food of most species is pollen and nectar, but fruits are also eaten. Until recently, the captive diet for these birds has consisted of 'nectar' made from such items as baby cereal and honey. When fed on this, the faeces are of a liquid consistency.

Some breeders are now giving a dry diet, at least for part of the day. While the hardier species will exist on this, the delicate ones, such as the Fairy Lorikeet (*Charmosyna pulchella*), and the more conservative feeders, such as the *Chalcopsitta* lories, would starve to death rather than accept or even recognise dry items as food.

The experienced breeder should be most careful about the introduction of dry foods: the danger is that beginners will be misled into believing that all lories can be maintained on such foods. Pet store owners, or others anxious to sell lories, may try in this way to give the impression that their feeding is no more time-consuming or specialised than that of other parrots. Anyone not prepared to go to the trouble of providing nectar, should not consider keeping lories.

Some lories are among the most brilliantly coloured birds in existence – but they are not only colourful. Playful and lively in the extreme, they make fascinating aviary birds – showy, inquisitive, intelligent and often free-breeding. Although the clutch size of most species is only two, they make up for this by being multiple-brooded; three or four nests a year are not uncommon. Breeders who crave the excitement of the breeding season all year round would do well to consider lories. However, young have to be hand-reared during cold weather, which they are otherwise unlikely to survive during the first few days of life.

Each pair must have an enclosure to themselves, with the exception of the little Goldie's Lorikeet (*Trichoglossus goldiei*) which breeds well on the colony system. The larger species are dangerous companions for other birds. They have been known to kill wild birds or those from adjoining aviaries which have been unfortunate enough to find their way into the enclosure.

In lories, behaviour is not a reliable guide to sex. Two males or two females may be totally compatible and behave like a true pair. Sometimes two females will lay simultaneously, and only the appearance of four eggs indicates that the 'pair' consists of two females! Chromosome sexing is recommended; many captive lories are overweight due to incorrect feeding and lack of exercise, and sex is difficult to determine surgically in birds which are obese.

Suspended aviaries are the most hygienic way of maintaining lories, but they may not provide sufficient protection from the elements in a cold climate. In this case, walk-in aviaries, with a concrete floor and a drain in the middle, are recommended. They can thus be hosed down daily. Alternatively, shingle (large stones), to a depth of 15 cm (6 in), provides a surface which is easy to hose clean.

It is most important that lories have a nest-box for roosting at all times. The wood should be thick, to provide extra warmth on cold nights and because much gnawing occurs when the birds are breeding. Pieces of wood nailed inside, near the base, help the parents to keep the nest clean when chicks hatch. They gnaw at these to provide new nest litter.

If the nest is wet the chicks are almost certain to be plucked. The wood shavings used in the base of the nest must be changed as soon as they become damp; this might be as often as twice a week with large chicks. Holes drilled in the floor of the nest-box allow some of the liquid faeces to escape.

Nest hygiene is vitally important with lories. A damp nest may become a breeding ground for bacteria. Often the parents are blamed when chicks die, but their death could be due to bacterial infection. Between each clutch, the nest-box should be emptied, sterilised and then filled, to a depth of at least 5 cm (2 in), with clean shavings.

The most critical stage in the rearing period is when the female ceases to brood the chicks, before they are fully feathered. In Britain, for example, nearly all winter-hatched chicks die between six and ten days unless removed for hand-rearing at an early age.

Young lories which fledge into outdoor aviaries should be put back in the nest at night if the weather is cold or damp – otherwise they may not survive the night. Sometimes they refuse to remain within the nest, in which case they can be placed in a cardboard box, or a small darkened cage, and kept indoors overnight and then returned to their parents early next morning.

There are several different genera of lories, the dietary requirements of which are discussed for each genus. However, they all consume 'nectar', the ingredients of which are described under that heading.

See also: *Chalcopsitta, Charmosyna, Eos, Glossopsitta, Lorius, Neopsittacus, Oreopsittacus, Phigys, Pseudeos, Trichoglossus, Vini.*

Lorius LORIES

Highly intelligent and playful birds, these are the largest of the lories in body size. They have heavy bodies and medium-length wide tails. In all species, the beak is orange. The length of those birds known to aviculturists is 28–31 cm (11–12 in).

Remarks on care and feeding under *Chalcopsitta* Lories apply also to the members of this genus, which are even more talented mimics, and more adventurous regarding choice of food. Many are very fond of greenfoods.

As is usual with lories, the clutch consists of two eggs, incubated by the female for about twenty-five days. The young spend about ten to eleven weeks in the nest, but widely differing fledgling periods have been reported.

The best-known members of the genus are the Chattering Lory (*L. garrulus garrulus*) and a

A Black-capped Lory (*Lorius lory lory*), aged thirty-four days.

sub-species, which differs only in having yellow on the mantle, the Yellow-backed Lory (*L. g. flavopalliatus*). They are beautiful birds, coloured scarlet with green wings and tail. Their personalities are equally flamboyant.

Less often available is the Black-capped Lory (*L. lory*), which differs from the Chattering in having the forehead and crown black, a wide blue band on the mantle and blue thighs and abdomen.

Be warned that these lories have very loud voices which are not usually considered pleasant!

LOVEBIRDS (*Agapornis*)

Lovebirds are ideal subjects for beginners interested in breeding, or, more correctly, certain species are, notably the Peach-faced, Masked and Fischer's. They are prolific, breed throughout the year and do not need large cages. They can be bred indoors (see *CAGES*), but hatchability is usually better out of doors.

Feeding is simple: a mixture of canary, millet and small sunflower

Parrakeets (2)

A pair of Horned Parrakeets *(Eunymphicus cornutus cornutus)* from New Caledonia.

Quaker Parrakeets *(Myiopsitta monachus)* feeding on palm fruits – a favourite food of many parrots.

The female
Moustached
Parrakeet *(Psittacula
alexandri fasciata)* is
distinguished by her
black upper
mandible.

seeds and a little hemp in winter. Spray millet is a great favourite. Apple, diced carrot and greenfood (seeding grasses, chickweed, spinach, etc.) are eaten, plus bread and milk when young are being reared. The more rarely kept Abyssinian differs slightly in that it needs more fruit.

Lovebirds originate from Africa (five species) and Madagascar (one species). The Black-collared (*A. swinderniana*) has never been kept alive in captivity, and the Abyssinian (*A. taranta*) and the Madagascar (*A. cana*) are not common, being difficult to breed in cold climates. The others are firm favourites with thousands of breeders, most of whom keep the Peach-faced (*A. roseicollis*) and its mutations.

This lovebird is about 15 cm (6 in) in length and plumage is alike in male and female. The original wild type is green, with the face and throat salmon pink and the rump and tail coverts bright blue. Immature birds have softer colours and brownish (not horn-coloured) upper mandibles. Many, many mutations and their combinations are being bred. Young of several different colours can be produced in one nest.

Because it builds a nest (provide willow twigs for lovebirds to strip the bark, and also grasses), the nest-box needs to be larger than usual for a bird of its size: it should measure approximately $23 \times 15 \times 17$ cm high ($9 \times 6 \times 7$ in).

Females carry material into the nest tucked into the feathers of the rump; males do not usually do this. Another indication of sex is clutches of ten eggs or more: a 'pair' of two females laying simultaneously! The usual clutch size is about five and the incubation period twenty-three days. Newly hatched chicks have dark pink down. The young spend about six weeks in the nest.

The Masked Lovebird (*A. personata personata*) is unmistakable, with its black head and yellow breast; the wings are green. Immature birds are less brightly coloured and have black at the base of the upper mandible. A conspicuous area of white skin surrounds the eye. Length is 15 cm (6 in). There is a very popular blue mutation, in which the green areas are replaced by blue and the yellow by greyish-white. Breeding and

management are as described for the Peach-faced, except that colony breeding is not carried out.

Yellow Fischer's Lovebirds: the Fischer's, like the Masked and the Black-cheeked Lovebirds, have a white eye-ring.

The Black-cheeked Lovebird (*A. p. nigrigenis*) varies in availability; in Britain it is uncommon, yet in some European countries (Denmark, for example), many are bred. It differs from the Masked in having the top of the head brown, the upper breast pale salmon in colour.

Fischer's Lovebird (*A. p. fischeri*) has the forehead, cheeks and throat orange-red, upper breast and neck yellow, rump and tail coverts blue and the tail tipped with lighter blue. The top of the head is smokey-brown. It is slightly smaller than the Masked. Several mutations are being bred.

The Nyasa Lovebird (*A. p. lilianae*) differs from the Fischer's in lacking blue on the tail and rump and in its slightly smaller size – 13 cm (5¼ in). There is a rare and extremely beautiful lutino mutation, which is pure yellow with the delicate pinkish-orange head colour retained. The Nyasa breeds well on the colony system, but is rare in aviculture in most countries, although well established in New Zealand, Australia and California. A winter breeder, it does better in a warm climate.

The Madagascar Lovebird (*A. cana*) can be sexed as soon as it feathers, the male having the head and breast grey, the upperparts dark green and the underparts light green. The beak is pale grey. The female is dark green above and slightly more yellowish-green below than the male.

M

MACAWS (*Ara*)

Because of their intelligence and individuality, macaws are among the most fascinating of aviary birds. They include the largest and most spectacular members of the parrot family (see under *HYACINTHINE MACAW* for members of the genus *Anodorhynchus*). Most macaws are included in the genus *Ara*, whose members vary greatly in coloration and size – from about 86 cm (34 in) to only 34 cm (13 in). Weight varies from well over 1,000 g (35 oz) in the Green-winged Macaw, to about 165 g (6 oz) in the smallest, the Hahn's. The feature that all the *Ara* species have in common is an area on the cheeks which is almost bare, being decorated with lines of tiny feathers in the larger species.

Undoubtedly many people have been drawn to parrot keeping by the desire to own a large macaw. Alas, these flamboyant birds have often attracted those with more money than sympathy. It is not unknown for wealthy people to choose a macaw to match the decor of their home!

Macaws are extremely sensitive birds; they need to be with their own kind, but if kept alone as a pet it is essential that they are among those who understand them. If not, their lives are miserable and they develop unfortunate habits, such as screaming or plucking themselves.

In any case, keeping a large macaw in a home creates many problems. These birds are extremely noisy, with far-carrying voices. It is impossible to keep one without furniture or furnishings being damaged, so the house-proud, and those with close neighbours, or intolerant family members, can rule out the idea of a pet macaw. So can those who do not spend much time at home. Macaws are simply too demanding for the average person to cope with.

Except for the very fortunate minority who are able to keep macaws at liberty, the only practical method is housing them in an aviary. Suspended or traditional types of cages can be used – and the larger the better. Many macaws kept in aviaries do not attempt to fly because the enclosure is simply too small. There is nothing as satisfying as seeing a macaw in flight, even if only over a short distance. A flight 8 m (26 ft) long is therefore recommended for the large species.

Regrettably, many breeding pairs are kept in enclosures so small the birds have no opportunity to exercise their wings. This practice will eventually lead to very poor specimens being produced. Macaws *must* be able to exercise their wings fully. The need to do so is evident at an early age – in young birds being hand-reared at weaning stage, for example. When removed from their cage they flap their wings vigorously for a long time; other parrots also do this, but for a few seconds only.

The large macaws are truly omnivorous and will consume a wide range of foods. They have a need for hard foods such as nuts (especially Brazils, walnuts and raw coconut) and can also be given stones to grind and play with. Seed and the smaller nuts, such as peanuts and pine nuts, should form no more than 50% of the diet. These can include sunflower, safflower, buckwheat, oats or groats, wheat and hemp, and also spray millet. Fresh fruit and vegetables (cooked beans and other vegetables can also be offered) should form about 30% of the diet. The larger species should be offered animal protein to stimulate breeding and when young are in the nest. A chop bone or chicken carcase is especially relished.

The small macaws, often known as dwarf macaws, have less need for animal protein. Their nuts will need to be cracked or halved and canary seed and millet can be added to their seed mixture.

Macaws are impossible to sex by outward appearance, and surgical or chromosome sexing is recommended. Possibly more same-sex 'pairs' have been kept together by owners convinced that they had a true pair, than in any other group of parrots. A strange phenomenon in three species is the imbalance in the sex ratio: by far the majority of Scarlet Macaws in

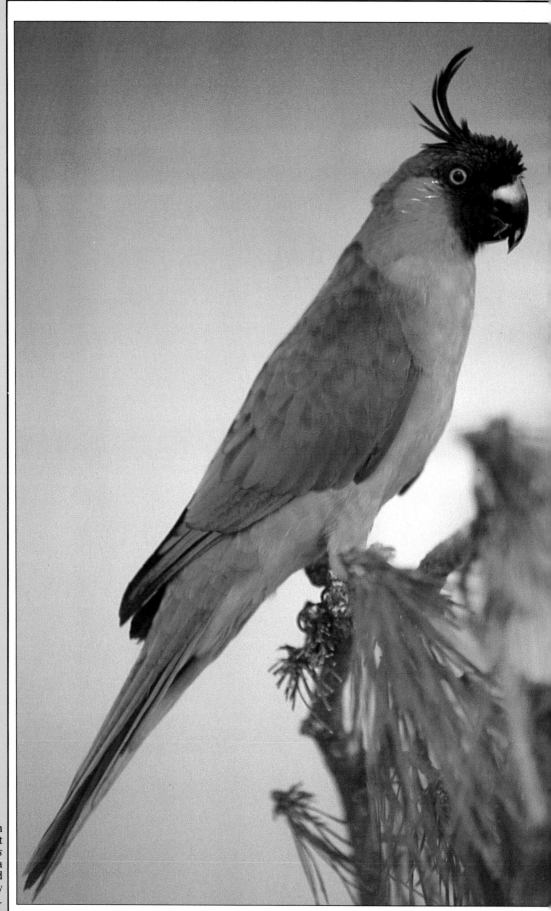

A male Uvaeen
Parrakeet
*(Eunymphicus
cornutus uvaeensis)* a
highly endangered
species with a very
small habitat.

Parrakeets (3)

A Port Lincoln Parrakeet (*Barnardius zonarius zonarius*).

An Amboina King Parrakeet *(Alisterus amboinensis amboinensis)* from the islands of Amboina and Ceram in Indonesia.

The male Alexandrine Parrakeet *(Psittacula eupatria)* has an enormously long tail. A single feather can measure as much as 36 cm (14 in).

captivity are males, there are more Green-winged males than females, and in the Blue and Yellow Macaw, females predominate.

This explains why there are so many couples consisting of a male Scarlet and a female Blue and Yellow and is one reason why so many hybrid macaws are reared. In the USA hybrids are popular, and may even sell for more than pure species, and so the various crosses have been given different names. Hybridising, however, unless there is a very good reason for it, is to be condemned, especially in the case of the large macaws because they are endangered in the wild.

Compatibility is of extreme importance in breeding macaws: owning a male and a female of the same species is not enough. If the birds do not like each other, it is a waste of time persevering. Although I condemn hybrid breeding, it must be admitted that often a large macaw will fall instantly in love with a bird of another species, and then the owner does not have the heart to part the devoted couple. Such situations are best avoided.

The large macaws can be dangerously aggressive when breeding. The nest-box should, therefore, be situated where it can be inspected from outside the aviary. A barrel on its side can be used as a nest site, but it should not be too large. It is best mounted outside the aviary for ease of inspection.

When macaws become noisier and more aggressive than usual, breeding can be expected. The clutch size in the large species (Red-fronted Macaw and upwards in size) is two to four, and the incubation period is twenty-four to twenty-eight days. Incubation is carried out by the female, but many males spend long periods inside the nest. The young fledge after about ninety to ninety-five days, but there is considerable variation in this period.

Many macaws are excellent parents and look after their young perfectly. Rearing from the egg by the breeder is not recommended except in an emergency. If the parents refuse to feed the young, I prefer to foster them under other macaws or even *Aratinga* conures. The only disadvantage of parent-reared chicks is that they

are much more difficult to tame. However, if placed in a small aviary when they are independent and can be removed from their parents, most will become tame after a few weeks.

All macaws should be provided with a rearing food when chicks are in the nest. This can consist of a proprietary food with the addition of hard-boiled egg, or a mixture of wholewheat bread with grated carrot, chopped up greenfood and hard-boiled egg and a little peanut butter, for example.

A cooked rearing food, used with success by one breeder, consisted of four cups each of chicken scratch and rice and eight cups of water, cooked for about 45 minutes. To this was added ¼ cup of Karo syrup, six cups of parrot mixture and 450 g (1 lb) each of sweetcorn and frozen mixed vegetables. Sometimes four cups of dog food or monkey chow were added, plus brewers' yeast, bone meal, cod liver oil and vitamins. This quantity lasted ten macaws for three or four days.

Macaws enjoy bread, biscuits, fresh corn on the cob (an excellent weaning food) and a wide variety of items from the table, cooked and uncooked.

The large *Ara* species most likely to be encountered are the Blue and Yellow (*A. ararauna*), Green-winged (*A. chloroptera*) and the Scarlet (*A. macao*). The former, often known as the Blue and Gold, is mainly rich skyblue above and yellow below. The length, including the long tail (about half the total) is about 85 cm (34 in). This is one of the most free-breeding macaws and can be recommended to those who have not previously kept large macaws. It is the most numerous in captivity and one of the most plentiful in the wild. It occurs throughout tropical South America and Panama.

Approximately the same area of distribution is shared by the Green-winged Macaw; it is about the same total length but considerably larger in body size and greater in weight. It has the most massive head and bill of any macaw except the Hyacinthine. Plumage is mainly crimson on the head and underparts, dark green on the wings and light blue on the back, rump and tail coverts. This is an under-rated species which has never achieved the popularity of the now much more expensive Scarlet.

The latter is often considered to be the most beautiful member of the genus, with its fiery scarlet plumage set off by the yellow on the centre of the wing and the light skyblue back, rump and upper tail coverts. The facial skin is bare of markings. In length it is about 90 cm (36 in).

In all the large macaws, young birds can be distinguished by the indistinct greyish colour of the iris of the eye, lighter coloration of the beak and, on fledging, by the shorter tail.

The Military Macaw (*Ara militaris mexicana*) from Mexico is much more common in the USA than in Europe. It has dense, short, red feathers on the forehead, its chin is brown and its rump and upper tail coverts are light blue. The tail feathers are maroon, tipped with blue above. The plumage is otherwise mainly an olive shade of green. In length it is about 70 cm (28 in).

Buffon's Macaw (*Ara ambigua)* reaches a length of 82 cm (33 in). The upper side of the tail is more orange-red than maroon.

Both these macaws have the bare skin on their faces, decorated with lines of tiny red and blackish-brown feathers. The sheer size of the largest Buffon's Macaws makes them imposing birds. The Military, seldom kept as a pet, is an extremely attractive aviary bird.

There are six small species of *Ara* macaws which are often given the name of dwarf macaws. They make enchanting pets, especially if hand-reared, being highly intelligent, playful and affectionate. They will also learn to mimic a few words. Their voices are loud and harsh and they are, of course, destructive, but the smallest, such as the Hahn's, can be very highly recommended as pets if obtained when young.

As aviary birds they are delightful, being hardy (with the exception of the Red-bellied, *A. manilata*), inquisitive and often extremely free-breeding. I know of a pair of Illiger's (*A. maracana*) in England which reared seventy-nine young between February 1978, when obtained, and April 1986 when I last heard from their owner! These young were reared totally by their parents.

The small macaws generally lay three or four eggs which are incubated by the female for between twenty-four and twenty-six days. The young spend thirteen or fourteen weeks in the nest.

The dwarf macaws consist of the following species: Yellow-collared, also called the Yellow-naped (*A. auricollis*), which measures about 40 cm (16 in); Severe Macaw (*A. severa*), also called the Chestnut-fronted Macaw, which is 49 cm (19 in) long; Hahn's (*A. nobilis nobilis*) and the Noble Macaw (*A. n. cumanensis*). One species, Coulon's (*A. couloni*) is unknown in captivity, and the Red-bellied is extremely susceptible to stress and recommended only for the most experienced macaw keepers.

Micropsitta – see *PYGMY PARROTS*

MOULTING

Parrots normally moult once a year, each individual usually moulting at about the same time each year. Stress or shock can bring on a partial or premature moult. In a severe case of shock, most of the flight feathers could be moulted in a few hours, or a partial moult of various feathers could occur. Normally, the moult is a gradual process; only one or two flight feathers being moulted at the same time, so that the bird's flight capability is not impaired.

Dishonest persons, attempting to sell a parrot which has plucked itself, or one which is suffering from PB and FDS may claim that the bird is moulting, but under normal circumstances there is little apparent loss of feather during this process. Except that some birds have a number of head feathers in quills (because they have no companion to preen their head feathers, or belong to a species in which mutual preening does not occur), or that missing flight feathers may be noticed when the wing is stretched, the moult should not be very obvious.

The duration of the moult varies according to the individual and species. Some of the larger parrots can take two months to moult completely, apart from the flight feathers, which are renewed over a

Macaws

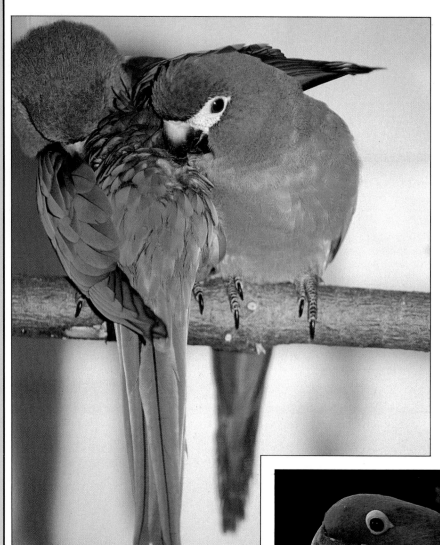

Hyacinthine Macaws *(Anodorhynchus hyacinthinus)* – the largest and one of the most magnificent of parrot species.

Blue and Yellow Macaws *(Ara ararauna)* are the most commonly kept and bred of the large *Ara* species.

The Green-winged Macaw *(Ara chloroptera)* is perhaps the most under-rated of the large macaws.

much longer period. Not all the flight feathers are renewed every year, thus it may be two years before a parrot, received with cut wings, has re-grown every feather. Pet owners who clip their birds' wings must check the state of regrowth. It could happen that the bird will moult soon after clipping, and the owner may be unprepared for the fact that very soon it will again be capable of flight.

Birds which are moulting need moisture on their plumage even more than at other times of year. Pet owners should be sure to spray them with warm water, every day if possible. The growing feather is encased in a whitish sheath which can become quite hard without moisture.

This protective sheath gradually disintegrates. Occasionally, however, it fails to do so, and then it hardens and prevents the feather from opening. When this occurs on a tail or flight feather, the sheath should be softened with warm water and gently removed. Unless this is carried out soon after the sheath should have normally disintegrated, the feather will be useless. If several feathers are affected in this way, it is usually an indication that the bird is in poor condition. A vitamin and mineral additive should then be added to a favourite item of food two or three times a week for several weeks, to try to correct any deficiency in the diet.

It is natural for a bird to scratch frequently when moulting and to preen vigorously, thus releasing a considerable amount of feather debris and dead skin. The skin on the feet, and also that to which the contour feathers are attached, is also renewed about once a year.

The age at which the first moult occurs varies according to the species. In small species, it may be only a few weeks after they have fledged; in larger parrots, such as Amazons and macaws, the first moult occurs at the age of about nine or ten months. However, the time of year when the bird hatched may influence this.

Feathers are composed of protein, and increasing the amount of protein in the diet, or giving animal protein (see entry) before and during the moult, must aid the production of good quality feather.

N and O

Nandayus CONURE

The reason why the single member of this genus, the Nanday Conure (*Nandayus nenday*), has been separated from the *Aratinga* conures is not clear. Its care and breeding are the same as recommended for the members of the *Aratinga* genus.

This species is identified by its black head and black beak. In length it is about 31 cm (12 in). The throat and upper breast are blue and the thighs are red.

It originates from Brazil, Bolivia, Paraguay and northern Argentina, where it occurs in large flocks.

This species has a reputation for being very noisy. However, it is very free-breeding, and the hand-reared young are much quieter and make delightful and affectionate pets.

Nannopsittaca PARROTLETS

This genus contains two species, one of which was discovered as recently as October 1985. While working in the Manu National Park in Peru, Dr Charles A. Munn observed a small parrotlet which he was unable to identify – five individuals in all. The following year he repeatedly observed flocks of the same species at a location 30 km further downstream. It has since been observed by other ornithologists in an unexplored region east of the Peruvian city of Pucallpa, near the Brazilian border. Still unnamed, it appears to belong in this genus, being bright green, with powder-blue forecrown, flesh coloured bill and feet and a faint light iris of the eye.

The Tepui Parrotlet (*N. panychlora*) is all green, except for yellow around the eye, especially under it. The tail is short and square, the bill is dusky and the iris is brown. Length is about 14 cm (5½ in). This species originates from southern Venezuela, in the Pantepui region adjacent to extreme western Guyana. It occurs only on the summits and slopes of isolated mountains and most of its habitat is inaccessible, which accounts for it being totally unknown in aviculture. It is apparently not rare, being seen in large flocks in the only part of its range which is easily accessible.

A flock was encountered by a Guyanese explorer making an unsuccessful attempt to scale the precipitous face of a mountain in the Pacaraima range. Base camp was establshed at 2,100 m (7,000 ft); above it the mountain rose sheer for 540 m (1,800 ft) to the summit. The little parrots could be heard at this point every morning and evening, moving to and from their feeding grounds in the forest below. Their flights took them through the cumulus cloud level. Almost continuous mist and cloud prevented the observers from actually seeing the birds which, it was believed, could have numbered several thousands.

Assuming that the new species is a *Nannopsittaca*, this genus is the least known of all neotropical parrots.

NECTAR

Many different ingredients can form the liquid food given to lories, known as nectar. The basis is usually baby cereal and honey or glucose, plus, except in a warm climate, a little baby milk or condensed milk. One can purchase nectar mixtures in powder form. Several kinds are excellent, but they tend to be expensive and therefore out of the question for most people who keep more than half a dozen lories. For this reason, most breeders make up their own mixture. The consistency should be runny and the ingredients should not be too rich; large quantities of milk and cereal could result in overweight birds and fatty degeneration of the liver.

The mixture I have used for many years is made as follows: approximately 36 g (about one large tablespoon or two dessertspoonfuls) of malt extract and 36 g of honey (or glucose) are dissolved in 400 ml (15 fl oz) of still-hot, boiled water. Then 25 g (2–3 tablespoonfuls or 4 dessertspoonfuls) of baby cereal are added and stirred, and hot and cold water added to make about 2 litres (70 fl oz) of nectar. Many baby cereals are suitable; I prefer one of the numerous fruit-flavoured kinds. The mixture is fed warm because this is how lories prefer it! Various fruits, or carrot, liquidised in a blender, are added on occasions, and also a vitamin and mineral supplement, although more rarely.

Other items which can be used are malted drinks such as Horlicks, invalid foods such as Complan (there is a strawberry-flavoured kind), baby rice (dry form), wheat germ cereal (if made into a flour in a food mixer or blender) and jars of apple sauce or fruit dessert baby foods bought in jars and tins.

Most nectar separates after a few hours, so this should be fed twice daily. There is a move now towards feeding lories mainly on dry foods. However, some species could not exist on such a diet, and until the long-term effects of this are known, I would hesitate to recommend it.

Neophema **PARRAKEETS** – see *GRASS PARRAKEETS*

Neopsittacus **LORIES**

The two small lorikeets which comprise this genus come from New Guinea. Unusually among lories, they have, on the underparts, a shade of red which one associates with neotropical parrots rather than lories – a dark red like a Green-winged Macaw. The beak is extremely strong, indicating that in the wild they feed on seed more extensively than other lories. In captivity, seed should form at least 50% of the diet.

Musschenbroek's Lorikeet (*N. musschenbroekii*) measures 23 cm (9 in). The head is green, streaked with yellow, and the crown and nape are brown (browner in the male). The underparts are irregularly marked with red, and the underside of the tail is orange-yellow, with yellow at the tip. The beak is orange and the eye red. Immature birds have only a tinge of red on their underparts.

This species was almost unknown in aviculture until the late 1970s; no commercial importations reached Britain until 1986. By this time, they had been bred in Germany and Denmark, but were not well established. Most of the birds available to date have been wild-caught and are very nervous. Unlike most lories, they seem to take a long time to settle down in captivity.

The diet should consist of a mixture of small seeds, such as groats, hemp, white millet and canary (they will also eat paddy rice, pumpkin seeds and small pine nuts). Millet spray should be given frequently, preferably daily, as this is greatly relished. Their very strong beaks can even deal with cracked walnuts! (I had mine a year before I discovered their liking for these.) They also like corn on the cob, sweet corn kernels, carrot, apple, soaked dried figs, orange, soaked sultanas and soaked sunflower seed. If offered a suitably varied diet, they will consume only a small amount of nectar.

For their size, they have, perhaps, more powerful beaks than any other parrot. At all costs, avoid being bitten by a Musschenbroek's Lorikeet! They are extremely destructive to woodwork and should be provided with fresh branches for gnawing at least once a week. They are also adept at opening doors which are not properly secured.

The clutch size is two eggs, incubated for about twenty-four days by the female.

The Alpine or Emerald Lorikeet (*N. pullicauda*) differs from Musschenbroek's in its smaller size, being 18 cm (7 in). It also has a more extensive area of red on the breast, and the nape is only tinged with brown. Occasionally, a single bird of this species has been found in a consignment of Musschenbroek's. Lory enthusiasts are ever on the look out for them, as they are extremely rare in captivity.

NEST SITES IN THE WILD

It is well known that the majority of parrots nest in holes in trees, but there are some interesting exceptions. This depends more on the locality in which the bird occurs, than on the species. An excellent example is the Bahaman Amazon Parrot (*Amazona leucocephala bahamensis*), a race of the Cuban Amazon. It is now confined to two islands.

On Inagua it nests in trees, but on Abaco the only trees are pines and most are too small for nest sites. Here, therefore, the parrots use underground cavities in limestone rocks.

A number of species of macaws, Amazons and conures nest in holes in rock faces. In captivity, many macaws choose to nest on the ground. Unusual nest sites chosen by Amazons in the wild include the stone wall of an ancient Mayan temple in Guatemala and an old chimney on the island of St Vincent in the Caribbean.

Parrots in three regions – Australia, Africa and South America – have discovered what useful nesting sites are termitaria – the homes of termites. In Central America, the Half-moon Conure (*Aratinga canicularis*) is so dependent on these that its distribution is directly related to that of the termites. After hollowing out their nest in the termitarium, the conures desert it until the termites have sealed up the entrances from the tunnels leading to the conures' chamber.

Apart from termitaria being easily excavated sites, parrots set up home near termites because of the protection the latter offer against nest predators. Most termites' nests are situated in trees, but they may also be built on ground. In Australia, huge free-standing termitaria, in the tropical Cape York region, harbour nests of the Golden-shouldered Parakeet (also known as the Anthill Parrot). The high temperature within, during the day, results in the female ceasing to incubate for several hours and also leaving the young unbrooded. Aviary-breeding of this species therefore presents a unique problem which has been overcome by providing electrically heated nest-boxes.

In Africa, the little Red-faced Lovebird (*Agapornis pullaria*) uses termitaria in trees and on the ground. This species has very rarely been bred in captivity, but success has occurred using a specially constructed bale of peat or nest-box packed with peat to simulate a termitarium.

Other lovebird species are very much less specialised in their nesting requirements. The Peach-faced, for example, has been known to use crevices in buildings and, more commonly, to take over weavers' nests. Among the most prolific birds in the world, weavers breed in colonies containing thousands, or hundreds of thousands of nests.

In the neotropics, small parrots

in arid localities, in which trees are scarce or non-existent, nest in cacti. A correspondent in Argentina once described to me nests of the little Aymara Parrakeet (*Bolborhynchus aymara*). Located within a cactus, surrounded by low spiny bushes, he described this as a 'truly impenetrable combination'. Another member of the same genus from Argentina, the Mountain Parrakeet (*B. aurifrons*), has been known to form a nest by burrowing into an earth bank. In captivity, this species will use an ordinary nest-box.

Two of the best-known parrots which do not use holes in trees are the Quaker Parrakeet and the Patagonian Conure (see under *Cyanoliseus CONURE*).

Little is known of the nesting habits of lories outside Australia. Thane Pratt, of the Department of Biology at Rutgers University in the USA, made some interesting suggestions on this subject. After noticing certain small species in New Guinea exploring the thick moss 'cushions' draped over tree limbs in the forest canopy, he continued to watch with interest. He saw Fairy Lorikeets climbing into one of these cushions (they may be several feet thick and support small 'gardens' of orchids and ferns), and Josephine's Lorikeets were also seen leaving a clump of epiphytes from which chicks were heard calling.

According to people of the Huon Peninsula, Papuan Lorikeets choose to nest in the massive accumulations of dead leaves in the crowns of *Pandanus* palms. In captivity, all small lorikeets readily accept a nest-box, except the Goldie's, many of which are reluctant to enter a box.

Little is known of the nesting habits of many species of parrots, so one must bear in mind that their nest sites are not necessarily holes in trees!

NEST-BOXES

Nest-boxes should be constructed of wood, not of a synthetic material such as plastic, or from metal. It is true that plastic would be easy to keep clean, but breeding parrots must be able to gnaw at the inside of their nest. Initially, this nest preparation stimulates egg-laying. The interior is gnawed away to provide a suitable surface for the eggs. When the chicks hatch, the material gnawed from the interior of the nest assists in keeping it dry and sanitary.

The faeces of the chicks are not, of course, removed from the nest in hole-nesting birds, and thus fresh wood shavings must be added. Better still, pieces of wood should be nailed inside the box; this prolongs its life (an important consideration in view of the high cost of wood), reduces the likelihood of accidents as a result of the base of the nest being destroyed and prevents the breeder having to change or repair a nest which contains eggs or young.

The wood chosen must be waterproof; marine plywood is a good choice.

Metal is totally unsuitable for nesting sites. Despite this, some breeders do use metal dustbins for large destructive birds such as cockatoos. This is to be deplored; metal becomes unacceptably hot in summer and very cold in winter. Many parrots nest in the winter or use their box for roosting, and thus it must be cosy inside. Wood lined with welded mesh and with large pieces of wood screwed on (not nailed as projecting nails could cause serious injury) inside, is recommended.

To make the nest-box waterproof, roofing felt can be nailed to the top of the boxes of less destructive species. All nest-boxes should be placed where they are well shielded from the weather, if necessary by protecting the area with heavy plastic sheeting or polythene. By far the best site for the nest-box is outside the aviary, inside a covered passage, where nest inspection can be carried out in complete safety, regardless of the weather.

Except in a very shallow nest-box, it is essential to have a ladder leading from the nest entrance to the base. This can be made from wire or from wood – both have serious disadvantages and advantages. Several pieces of wood nailed horizontally are safest, provided that regular nest-inspection is carried out; these could be gnawed away, leaving a bird trapped inside. The other alternative is a ladder of welded mesh; it should be bent so that it bows out slightly, thus reducing the risk of a bird being trapped by its nails – a horrible fate. Every effort must be made to avoid this.

Given a choice, most parrots will choose smaller nests than those which breeders usually provide. In the wild, spacious nests are seldom available; indeed some are so small that, as the young grow, they have to stand on top of each other. As a general guide, the nest-box should be slightly longer than the length of the bird's body, minus its tail.

There are exceptions: the lovebird species, which carry material inside and build a bulky nest, need a box of twice this capacity. Also, birds known to lay very large clutches (such as some Rosellas, parrotlets and certain *Pyrrhura* conures) will also need a more spacious nest.

Some examples of nest-box sizes are as follows:

Cockatiel, 20 cm (8 in) square and 31 cm (12 in) high;

Grass Parrakeets (*Neophemas*), 18 cm (7 in) square and 31 cm (12 in) high;

Ringneck and similar sized *Psittacula* Parrakeets, 25 cm (10 in) square and 61 cm (2 ft) high;

Kakarikis, 20 cm (8 in) square and 31 cm (12 in) high;

Rosellas (*Platycercus*), 23 cm (9 in) square and 60 cm (2 ft) to 1.2 m (4 ft) high;

Goldie's Lorikeet, 13 cm (5 in) square and 23 cm (9 in) high;

Chattering Lory and Blue-fronted Amazon, 25 cm (10 in) square and 61 cm (2 ft) high;

Blue and Yellow Macaw, (horizontal) 39 cm (15 in) square and 105 cm (3 ft 6 in) long.

(Measurements given are internal dimensions.)

The nest entrance should be only just large enough to admit the species. If it is too large, there will be too much light inside. The entrance does not have to be round or centrally positioned. Anyone who possesses a saw, but not a drill, will find that a square entrance hole in the corner of the nest is just as acceptable to the birds; indeed, they probably prefer it, as one corner of the nest will always be in darkness.

Regarding nest inspection, bear in mind that birds panic when a hand approaches them from above, cutting off their only means of escape. Inspection should be via a hinged flap in the side. Do not make this flap tight-fitting, or when the wood becomes damp it will expand. Ensure that there is a secure and easily operated catch to keep it closed; use a padlock where there is any opportunity for theft.

The perch below the nest entrance can be made from dowelling or from a short piece of natural wood (from fruit trees, plane, elm, poplar, etc.). It should extend a little way inside the nest, as many males like to sit at the entrance when their females are incubating.

The nest-box must be sited where it can be inspected without entering the aviary.

Wood shavings, or a mixture of this material and peat, are suitable for the base of the box. Be careful about the source of the wood shavings: those obtained from a timber merchant may contain wood which has been treated with a preparation which is harmful to birds. The best source is the packed litter sold in pet shops.

The position of the nest-box will depend on a number of factors, such as prevailing winds and the need for a sheltered location. For birds which breed in spring and summer, it is usually best to place it in the outside flight with immediate overhead cover. For some winter breeders, such as lovebirds, it may be best to place it in the shelter, but bear in mind that hatchability may be higher in an outdoor location.

For aggressive birds, those which

are nervous, and for females who rush back to the nest before one can reach it, the nest-box must be positioned to coincide with an inspection door in the side of the aviary, or opening on to a service passage. If nest inspection is difficult, breeding results will be poor. It is essential to know what is happening within the nest.

Barrels are sometimes used as nests for cockatoos and macaws. The disadvantage is that it is difficult to position them in such a way that nest inspection can occur from outside the aviary, unless they are built into the side of the enclosure when it is first constructed.

For seasonal breeders and those which do not roost in their boxes, the nest-boxes should be removed or boarded up out of the breeding season. Their later return, or opening up, will then act as a stimulus to breeding.

NET

A net for catching birds is an essential piece of equipment for those who keep birds in aviaries or suspended cages. It should be one that is designed for the purpose, not a fish net, for example. It should have a padded rim to prevent possible injury and the material must be suitable. Cotton is best, not nylon or a mesh in which the bird's claws could become entangled. The material should be a neutral colour or a dark one, such as brown, not white or a bright shade.

Anyone who keeps parrot species ranging from the largest to the smallest, should have nets of three different sizes, the diameters being approximately 18 cm (7 in), 25 cm (10 in) and 36 cm (14 in). Because of the difficulty in catching birds in suspended cages, nets with extra long handles are necessary.

It is generally easier and quicker to catch a bird when it is flying, as when it is clinging to the wire one has the additional task of releasing beak and feet. To avoid being bitten through the net, grasp the bird's head with thumb and forefinger on either side of the mandibles so that it cannot manoeuvre its head to bite. The claws can then be released.

Always keep the catching nets in the same place so that in an emergency you do not have to search for them. Also ensure that they are kept in good repair.

NIGHT PARROT (*Geopsittacus occidentalis*)

Nocturnal and almost certainly nomadic, the Night Parrot has been described as the most mysterious of Australian birds. Only one specimen has been collected this century (no longer in existence) and there are only two reliable reports of it having been seen. Found only in the interior, it must have declined greatly, and may already be extinct in the eastern part of its range, from where there have been no records for more than sixty years.

Great was the excitement in June 1979, therefore, when four birds were sighted at Coopers Creek in far north-eastern South Australia. This occurred in a vast area of undisturbed habitat. One bird was flushed by approaching camels, rising up about 30 m (100 ft) in front of the camels and flying 4 or 5 m (12–15 ft) close to the ground. Then people on foot disturbed three more birds at the base of a bush. They flew at a height of 3–4 m (10–12 ft) before dropping down into dense vegetation.

What a wonderful moment it must have been for the ornithologists who sighted these birds – to have proof at last that the species still survived.

The Night Parrot is small, about 23 cm (9 in) long, with a short, gradated tail. It is yellowish-green, mottled with brown, black and yellow. The bill is horn-coloured

Nest sites for macaws, such as this barrel, should be mounted outside the aviary for ease of inspection.

and the iris is black. It is closely associated with spinifex (*Triodia*). *The Atlas of Australian Birds* states: 'A study of the records in South Australia concludes that samphire flats associated with lake systems may be important to the survival of the Night Parrot, perhaps specially between years of heavy rain; when rain brings the spinifex into flower and the seeds ripen, the parrot may move out from the lakes to the spinifex sandplains.'

There is only one credible record of this species in captivity. A single bird, caught in South Australia in 1867, was sent to London Zoo. It survived for four months, apparently dying of pneumonia in January 1968. In that era most parrots were kept in hot-house conditions, so it is surprising that it was apparently kept out of doors. Never again is this little-known bird likely to be seen outside Australia.

Ognorhynchus PARROT

Little is known about the single member of this genus, the Yellow-eared Parrot (*O. icterotis*), which has also been called a conure or parrakeet. In my opinion, it is most closely allied to the macaws. Its large bill and habit of 'blushing' are macaw-like, as is its general behaviour. In size and silhouette it is similar to the Thick-billed Parrot (*Rhynchopsitta*).

Its coloration is distinctive. The forehead, part of the crown, ear coverts and part of the cheeks are bright yellow. The tail is green above, dull maroon on the inner webs and pale maroon on the underside. The rest of the plumage is green, darker above and more yellowish-green below. The beak is black, as is the bare skin surrounding the eye. In length it is about 41 cm (16 in).

This species occurs only in the Andes of south-western Colombia and adjacent northern Ecuador, mainly between 2,300 and 3,000 m (7,550–9,850 ft). Regrettably, much of its former habitat has been deforested in recent years. A substantial population decline must have occurred, but this parrot has rarely been observed – let alone studied – so no population estimate is available. Much of its believed range in Ecuador is almost impossible of access, thus an undisturbed population may survive there.

The Yellow-eared Parrot is extremely rare in captivity. The only substantiated reports are of two birds received by a London dealer, on separate occasions, in 1965. One of these was later presented to Vogelpark Walsrode in Germany, after the owner had made repeated and unsuccessful attempts to purchase the other.

Opopsitta – see under *FIG PARROTS*

Oreopsittacus LORIKEET

The single member of this genus, the Alpine Lorikeet (*O. arfaki*), is unknown in aviculture. It has been collected on several occasions, but has proved impossible to keep alive for more than a few days. Thus it seems that this tiny parrot (15 cm/6 in) is unlikely to be available to breeders.

It is exquisitely and unusually coloured. The male has a red forehead and crown, and purple lores and cheeks, with two rows of white dots, or streaks, below the eye. His abdomen and lower flanks are yellow, red or green, and the under wing coverts and sides of the breast are red. The tail is green above and rose-red below. The plumage is otherwise mainly green.

The female has a green crown and forehead.

Uniquely among parrots, it has fourteen tail feathers (instead of twelve).

Found in the mountains of New Guinea, it has been observed there in small groups.

P

PALM COCKATOO – see under
BLACK COCKATOOS

PARROTLETS (*Forpus*)
Members of this genus are the
smallest parrots known in
aviculture, being smaller, on
average, than the lovebirds, their
African counterparts. The smallest
of the genus, the Spectacled
Parrotlet (*F. conspicillatus*)
measures only 11 cm (4½ in), and
the largest, the Yellow-faced (*F.
xanthops*), has a total length of 18
cm (7 in). All have very short tails.

They are basically light green,
the males having blue on the rump
and/or wings. The females of some
species are difficult to distinguish.

They originate in South and
Central America. There are seven
species: the Celestial (or Pacific),
Yellow-faced, Spectacled,
Blue-winged, Mexican, Guiana (or
Green-rumped) and Sclater's.

Parrotlets have many factors in
their favour. Being so small they
are inexpensive to feed and to
house. They are extremely quiet.
They nest readily and breed at a
very early age. The only major
problem with these little birds is
that, if closely confined, one bird
may kill another. Males may also
act aggressively towards young
males after fledging, and therefore
these youngsters should be
removed soon after they are able
to feed themselves properly. This
can be as soon as ten days after
leaving the nest.

Many parrotlets eat only seed,
but will sample bread and milk
when their chicks hatch. Their
staple diet should consist of the
usual range of small seeds (canary,
millet, groats, hemp and small
sunflower); fruit should also be
offered. Those at Loro Parque
relish the small orange fruits from
the palm trees there, which have a
fibrous exterior; they cannot eat
the hard nut in the centre. Other
foods sampled by parrotlets have
included spinach, seeding
forget-me-nots, moistened sponge
cake and also muesli cereal (oats,
wheatflakes, raisins, chopped nuts
and dates). Sprouted seed should

be given to those which will take
only seed.

A suitable nest-box would
measure about 18 cm (7 in) square
and 20 cm (8 in) high. Four to six
eggs are laid and incubated by the
female for about twenty to
twenty-three days. Chicks have
white down which is fairly sparse.
A distinctive feature is the bill
coloration which is mainly deep
pink.

Forpus chicks have the great
asset of being sexable as soon as
they feather up, at about three
weeks of age. They will consume
spray millet from the age of five or
six weeks and are independent by
eight weeks. They spend five weeks
in the nest.

PARROTLETS (*Touit*) – see
TOUIT PARROTLETS

**PATAGONIAN CONURE
(*Cyanoliseus patagonus*)**
This large and distinctively
coloured conure (which has a
feathered cere) is the only member
of the genus. There are three
sub-species, of which only the
Lesser (*C. p. patagonus*) is well
known in aviculture. It has the
head, upperparts and most of the
breast olive-green, olive-brown,
red and yellow on the abdomen
and thighs, and yellow on the rump
and tail coverts. Its length is 43–46
cm (17–18 in).

The much rarer Greater (*C. p.
byroni*) usually has a broken band
of white on the upper breast (the
Lesser has a little white at the sides
of the neck) and measures about 53
cm (21 in).

The Andean Patagonian Conure
(*C. p. andinus*) has little or no
yellow on the abdomen, less red,
and lacks the white near the neck.

The extremely loud and
far-carrying voice of this conure
rules it out of many collections.

Yellow-faced
Parrotlets and
other *Forpus*
species can be
sexed as soon as
the feathers
erupt.

This is regrettable, because it is a most attractive bird and breeds well in aviaries. Colony breeding is sometimes carried out but this is not recommended, as only the dominant pair may breed. On the other hand, keeping two pairs in one aviary apears to be a good arrangement.

At Loro Parque two pairs share the same enclosure nest simultaneously and make an excellent job of rearing the young. The clutch usually consists of three to five eggs which are incubated for twenty-four or twenty-five days. The young leave the nest at eight weeks. Obtained as soon as they are independent, they make the most delightful and affectionate pets, their loud voices being their only drawback.

The diet should be as recommended for *Pionus* parrots.

PESQUET'S PARROT (*Psittrichas fulgidus*)

This species is one of the most distinctive and aberrant of the parrots. A native of New Guinea, it is a fascinating bird, its large size and red and black plumage rendering it unmistakable.

It has a peculiar head (small and partly bare of feathers) and bill (elongated). Both these features must be adaptations for feeding on fruit. In captivity it is very noticeable that no seed or other hard foods are consumed, the hardest item being whole carrots. Fruit should not be cut into small pieces; instead, half a pear, half a banana and a large piece of papaya (a great favourite), for example, should be spiked onto a nail. Most fruits can be offered. One breeder made a porridge consisting of diced fruits, rolled oats, rice flour, breakfast cereals, milk powder, honey, calcium and vitamins.

Pairs rearing young must be offered protein: ground horsemeat and hard-boiled egg have been found acceptable. However, a chick which hatched at Loro Parque in my absence was reared for the first two weeks on nothing more than fruit, carrot and bread and milk. It was then removed for hand-rearing. It differed from parrot chicks of other species in its manner of gaping for food like a softbill. It was fed on the same food as other large parrots being hand-reared at the time, but its

A Pesquet's Parrot aged about eighty-four days. Note the natal down still adhering to the feathers of crown and nape, and the hair-like feathers on cheeks and ear coverts.

faeces were entirely different, being soft and cream-coloured. This proves that the digestive system is entirely different to that of omnivorous and seed-eating parrots.

Very intelligent, and aware of its surroundings, it was a fascinating chick to rear and never gave any problems. At about seventy-five days, it started to sample soft foods, including papaya and fresh corn on the cob.

This species lays two eggs, at intervals of three or four days. The female incubates for twenty-nine or thirty days. The young spend about fifteen weeks in the nest. At Loro Parque, nesting was stimulated by providing a palm log in which an entrance hole, about 10 cm (4 in) in depth, had been made. The male did most, or all, of the excavation, to a depth of about 1.2 m (4 ft), carrying out the excavated material in his plumage, so that every day there would be a pile on the ground near the log.

A Pesquet's Parrot (*Psittrichas fulgidus*), hand-reared at Loro Parque, aged about fifty-five days.

It is generally accepted that this species is sexually dimorphic; males have a few red feathers behind the eye. It appears, however, that young birds of both sexes show this colour, as has at least one adult female on record.

Pesquet's Parrots, although hardy in the sense that they tolerate cold weather, are extremely sensitive to change. Moving them to a new aviary should be avoided unless absolutely necessary. They are also susceptible to candidiasis.

Pezoporus wallicus – see *GROUND PARROT*

Phigys LORY

The single member of this genus is a beautiful small lory which has very rarely been kept in captivity outside Fiji. The Solitary, or Collared Lory (*P. solitarius*) has green wings and tail, and also a ruff of elongated bright green feathers on its nape, from which the name Collared Lory is derived. Its forehead, crown and abdomen are deep purple and the rest of the plumage is red. The iris of the eye, beak and legs are orange.

Immature birds have shorter feathers on their hind neck; the bill is brownish and the iris brown.

The length of this lory is 20 cm (8 in).

Found throughout the Fiji Islands, except in the Southern Lau group, the Collared Lory occurs in small groups in the vicinity of flowering trees, especially drala (*Erythrina indica*). It feeds on pollen and nectar. Common in some forested areas and the wetter, windward part of Viti Levu and Vanua Levu, it is less abundant in open and agricultural locations.

In the past, the Samoans and Tongans coveted the red feathers of this little parrot, which they used for edging mats. Since the trade in these feathers was officially prohibited, wool has been used, but the demand has not totally ceased.

Export of this species, and all other Fijian birds, is forbidden. In the past, the few who were fortunate enough to keep the Collared Lory wrote of it in glowing terms. The British aviculturist Sydney Porter, who, fifty years ago, owned many rare and beautiful parrots, described it as 'the loveliest and most engaging of the whole Parrot tribe'.

Food, in captivity, consists of nectar and fruit.

This species lays two eggs. The incubation period may be as long as twenty-seven days (twenty-five or twenty-six would seem more likely) and the young spend nine weeks in the nest.

PILEATED PARRAKEET
(*Purpureicephalus spurius*)

This parrakeet is the only member of its genus. It is easily recognised by its mauve breast, bright in the male and pale mauve in the female. The colour scheme is a most unusual one, especially the sharply contrasting tones of the male.

His ruby-red crown and forehead give rise to the name of Red-capped Parrot, by which the species is known in its native Australia. (The female's crown is brownish and green.) The male has lime-green cheeks, his dark green wings contrasting with his yellow rump and dark blue tail. The underside of the tail is light blue, tipped with white. The thighs and under tail coverts are scarlet. The male must surely be one of the most beautiful of all parrakeets, whereas the female's colours are duller.

Immature birds are less colourful than females, with pale red and green feathers on the under tail coverts.

The tail is long and gives a total length of 36 cm (14 in).

This species, found only in the south-western corner of Australia, is not common in aviculture, but is fairly common in the wild. It feeds mainly on the fruits of a certain kind of eucalyptus (*Eucalyptus calophylla*). Its bill has evolved its unusual shape (having a gap between the mandibles) in order that the bird can extract the seeds from the eucalyptus capsule. The curved lower mandible fits around the top of the capsule and the long upper mandible reaches inside to remove the seeds.

In captivity, Pileated Parrakeets relish the berries of hawthorn and pyracantha and, of course, branches of eucalyptus if available. If not, branches of fruit trees or pine should be provided, or much damage will be done to the aviary woodwork. The diet should consist of the usual seeds and much greenfood, such as chickweed, seeding grasses, sowthistle and the unripe heads of thistles. They eat more fruit than most Australian parrakeets. When rearing young they require bread and milk, or a proprietary rearing food, plus increased quantities of greenfood.

The clutch consists of four to seven eggs and the female commences incubation towards the completion of the clutch. Each egg is incubated for nineteen or twenty days. On hatching the chicks are covered in long white down. This is replaced by grey down with a white patch on the nape, as in the other broad-tailed parrakeets. The young spend about thirty-three days in the nest.

Although rather shy, this is a most active and attractive aviary bird. An enthusiastic bather, even recently fledged young will bathe, and a large, shallow water container should therefore be available.

Pionites – see under *CAIQUES*

Pionopsitta PARROTS

The six members of this genus are small parrots from South and Central America, measuring 21–25 cm (8–10 in). Only one species, the Red-capped (*P. pileata*), is known in aviculture. It is mainly green, with dull red on the ear coverts, and the bend of the wings and the primary coverts are deep blue. The male has a scarlet forehead and crown. This species originates from south-eastern Brazil, where it is endangered by deforestation, and from eastern Paraguay.

Food should consist of a seed mixture (sunflower, safflower, canary, millet, buckwheat, wheat and a little hemp and/or niger) and plenty of fresh fruits and vegetables. When chicks are in the nest, corn on the cob and a rearing food must be provided. Only three or four aviculturists have had consistent success with this species and the most successful is surely Tom Ireland in Florida. The rearing food he uses consists of wholemeal bread, grated carrot, chopped endive and vitamin and mineral supplements. He has found that the most successful method of breeding is to allow the birds to choose their own mates in a communal aviary. He then places bonded pairs in small suspended breeding cages.

Nesting commences in June. The clutch size is four or five and the incubation period is twenty-one to twenty-four days. The young spend about seven weeks in the nest.

This is a very sociable species, most likely to nest within sight or sound of others of its own kind. Its voice is pleasant – a soft warbling which could offend no one.

Pionus PARROTS

A group of small parrots from South and Central America, the *Pionus* are readily identified by their red under tail coverts. Most species are basically green, but two are unusual, one being dark blue and the other mainly brownish. They can be very highly recommended as aviary birds and as pets. They are small in size, often have very gentle natures and have quieter voices than Amazons or caiques, for example, making them very suitable to keep in the house. The size ranges from 24 cm (9½ in) to 29 cm (11 in).

Pionus will accept a very varied diet, which should include plenty of greenfood and vegetables, such as spinach, kale, cabbage, chickweed, sowthistle, celery, carrot and corn on the cob. Most will consume a lot of small seeds, such as canary, buckwheat and a little hemp. Sunflower and safflower seeds, peanuts and pine nuts are also enjoyed. Favourite foods include cracked walnuts, spray millet and hawthorn berries. All the usual fruits can be offered.

The plumage is alike in male and female and behaviour can be

A Blue-headed Pionus Parrot (*Pionus menstruus menstruus*). There is sometimes a hint of pink on the throat or, in the sub-species *rubrigularis*, a larger pink area.

misleading, so some form of sexing is recommended. Nest-boxes should be in the region of 29 cm (11 in) square and 36 cm (14 in) high, or smaller for the White-crowned. The clutch usually consists of three or four eggs, but occasionally two or even five. The female incubates for twenty-six days and the young spend about ten weeks in the nest.

Easily the best-known member of the genus is the Blue-headed (*P. menstruus menstruus*), instantly recognised by the rich dark blue of the head and upper breast.

The rare and endangered sub-species *reichenowi*, from coastal north-eastern Brazil, has a much paler shade of blue on the head, the underparts have a pale blue suffusion and the margins of the feathers of the under tail coverts are blue, not green as in the other sub-species.

This species has a very wide distribution, over most of tropical South America, and thus there is some variation in size and colour throughout the range, but size is generally about 28 cm (11 in).

The next most frequently available Pionus is Maximilian's (*P. maximiliani*) which is mainly an olive shade of green with, of course, red under tail coverts and, according to the sub-species, purplish blue, dark blue or vinous red on the throat and upper breast. In length it is 29 cm (11 in). Immature birds are duller and, as in most Pionus, may or may not have a band of red on the forehead. This species breeds well.

The Coral-billed (*P. sordidus corallinus*) differs from Maximilian's in its dark red beak, the inconspicuous area of greyish skin surrounding the eyes (white and very conspicuous in the Maximilian's) and in lacking the bronzy-green coloration on the wings.

The smallest member of the genus, the White-crowned (*P. senilis*), from Mexico and Central America, is occasionally available. It is recognised by its white crown, blue head and size, which is about 24 cm (9½ in). This species nests readily and some pairs prove quite prolific.

The other members of the genus are more rarely available and more expensive. The Dusky (*P. fuscus*), from the northern part of South America, is mainly brown with the breast in various shades of vinous or brighter red.

The Bronze-winged (*P. chalcopterus*) is mainly dark blue with white and pink feathers on the throat and bright, almost iridescent, light blue under the wings. Imported birds tend to have a nervous disposition, and to overpreen each other's heads.

The exquisite rich plum colour of the head of the Plum-crowned Pionus (*P. t. tumultuosus*) makes it extremely attractive. It occurs in the Andes of Bolivia and Peru and, as is usual with birds from high altitudes, it is not easy to establish in captivity.

The Massena's Parrot (*P. t. seniloides*), until recently considered as a separate species, is the rarest in captivity. It differs from the Plum-crowned in having the feathers of its head grey and white. It originates from north-western South America (Venezuela, Colombia, Ecuador and Peru).

Poicephalus PARROTS

The range of basic colours found in the African *Poicephalus* parrots is remarkable. Sexual dimorphism is either absent or marked, and in two species the female is more colourful than the male. Young or hand-reared birds make delightful pets; as aviary birds they are attractive and some pairs are quite prolific.

They could, perhaps, be described as the African counterparts of the *Pionus*, in that they are small (22–31 cm/9–12 in).

A good variety of foods should be offered: soaked sunflower seed, boiled maize, sprouted mung beans, peanuts, pine nuts, a mixture of small seeds, which may or may not be sampled, plenty of fresh fruits and vegetables (including corn on the cob when young are being reared) and cracked walnuts. Cape Parrots are passionately fond of the latter, and also like hawthorn berries. Bread and milk and/or a commercial rearing food, and even mealworms, will be accepted by birds rearing young.

Like some other African parrots in captivity, *Poicephalus* are usually winter breeders. In practice, this quite often means that the young have to be

107

hand-reared; however, they then make totally delightful pets. Most species are small and quiet which adds to their suitability as house pets. They are gentle and affectionate and may learn to repeat a few words. In contrast, many wild-caught *Poicephalus* are extremely nervous and suitable only as aviary birds.

Nest-boxes for the smaller species should be about 23 cm (9 in) square and 60 cm (24 in) high. Those for the Jardine's and Cape Parrot should be about 28 cm (11 in) square. The clutch consists of three or four eggs and the incubation period is twenty-six to twenty-eight days. Only the female incubates. The young spend ten to twelve weeks in the nest.

For many years the Senegal (*P. senegalus*) was the only readily available member of the genus. It has long been one of the most inexpensive of the true parrots – partly because many adults are imported and these are difficult to sell, being extremely nervous. This species has a grey head, the upperparts and breast green, and the abdomen yellow, matching the brilliant yellow eyes.

Immature birds are paler and have a black iris, changing to grey, then greyish-yellow.

The voice of this species is not very pleasant.

Second, regarding availability, is Meyer's Parrot (*P. meyeri*). It, too, is reasonably priced. The size is the same as the Senegal, being about 23 cm (9 in). Recognised by the yellow on the bend of its wing, thighs and under wing coverts, the plumage is otherwise mainly greyish-brown with the rump and underparts bluish-green or green. However, there are several sub-species which vary significantly; most have a yellow band on the crown and the rump may be green or blue. Immature birds are much duller and lack the yellow markings.

Despite its dull coloration, the Brown-headed Parrot (*P. cryptoxanthus*) can be recommended, especially young birds which make wonderful pets. Only 22 cm (8½ in) long, the plumage is mainly green with the head dusky brown and the under wing coverts yellow. The eye is a piercing yellow. Immature birds have a brown iris. Like the

Jardine's Parrot chick (*Poicephalus gulielmi*), one of the less frequently bred members of the genus.

Senegal, this species can be bred in a cage (minimum length 90 cm/3 ft), even indoors.

The unusually coloured Rüppell's Parrot (*P. rueppellii*) is less often available. The male is an almost uniform dark grey, with contrasting yellow shoulders, thighs and under wing coverts. The prettier female has the back, rump, upper tail coverts, lower abdomen and part of the thighs blue. The iris of the eye is a startling red in adults and brown in young birds, which resemble the females but are slightly less colourful than the females.

My own favourites are the Red-bellied and the Cape Parrot. The male of the former is exquisitely coloured. (I can never pass the aviary of the male at Loro Parque without stopping to admire him.) He is soft brown above with the lower breast, abdomen and under wing coverts orange and the rump soft green. All the colours are delicate. The beak and the skin surrounding the eyes are black, highlighting the red eyes. The female is very much duller, being soft brown, with the underparts and rump green.

Immature birds are like females, but the males have some orange feathers on their wing coverts and abdomen.

The only two species larger than 23 cm (9 in) are the Jardine's Parrot (*P. gulielmi*) and the Cape (*P. robustus*). Both have dark green body plumage, all the feathers of the wings being heavily margined with black in the former, whose head is green and black with the forehead orange, whereas in the Cape it is greyish or brownish (varying according to the sub-species) and usually only the female has orange on the forehead. The Cape is easily recognised by its enormous beak.

Both species tend to be nervous, the Cape Parrot exceptionally so. They do not easily adapt to captivity and even captive-bred birds can be very shy. Tame birds are charming, however. This species is threatened in the wild, seldom exported and reared in few collections. More effort must be made to establish it in captivity.

Polytelis PARRAKEETS

The three members of this genus are large, long-tailed parrakeets from Australia. Their elegant proportions, attractive colours and tameness have long made them favourites with breeders. One disadvantage, however, is their long periods of inactivity.

They are very easy to feed, accepting a mixture of the usual small seeds (canary, white millet, oats, wheat and a little hemp), plus sunflower seed and peanuts. Apple, carrot, spinach (or wild greenfoods, such as chickweed, seeding grasses and sowthistle) should also be offered daily. Berries of hawthorn, elder and mountain ash are relished.

Admired for its pastel colours and its renowned tameness, the Princess of Wales Parrakeet (*P. alexandrae*) is known as the Princess Parrot in Australia. Its coloration is extremely delicate and unusual and the two central tail feathers are greatly elongated, making up about half the total length of 45 cm (18 in) in the male. The female has a shorter tail, slightly duller coloration on the head, and greyish feathers on the rump, back and flanks. In the male this area is greyish-mauve. Both sexes have a pink throat, the forehead pale blue and the upper parts soft olive green. The wing coverts are yellowish-green.

Immature birds have shorter tails and duller plumage than the female. The crown colour is usually brighter blue in young males, who start to call and to erect the small feathers of the crown when several months old. Blue and lutino (yellow) mutations are being bred, but remain very expensive.

Although some pairs are good breeders, many are not, and thus the price of this species has never been low. Four to six eggs are laid and incubated for nineteen days. They spend five weeks in the nest.

This parrakeet is much better known in captivity than in the wild. Highly nomadic and rarely observed, little is known about it, but it is believed to be declining. According to *The Atlas of Australian Birds*, only one breeding episode involving many birds has been reported since 1933.

The Rock Pebbler Parrakeet (*P. anthopeplus*) is known as the Regent Parrot, or Smoker in Australia. Unusually coloured, the male is mainly yellow with red and bluish-black in the wings and olive on the mantle. The underside of the tail is black. The female is olive green and has the underside of the tail feathers margined with pink. The bill is coral-red. This species has the largest body size of the *Polytelis*, and measures about 41 cm (16 in). Immature birds are more like the female although young males are usually of a yellower shade. Adult plumage is obtained by about fifteen months. Breeding usually commences at two years.

This species is a very strong flyer and will make good use of a long flight – at least 5 m (15 ft) in length. Some pairs will not enter a nest-box, but will make a depression on the aviary floor (if made of soil or turf). As long as protection from the elements is provided, this need not be discouraged. Four eggs are laid and incubated by the female for about twenty days. The young spend five weeks in the nest.

The male Barraband's Parrakeet (*P. swainsonii*) is an extremely striking bird with a yellow face bordered by a crescent of red. Its colouring and proportions are extremely elegant. The female is mainly green, of a less vivid shade than the male; the throat feathers are margined with pink, as are the outer tail feathers.

Immature birds are much like the female, but have a brown iris – not yellow as in adults.

The clutch size is four or five.

Prioniturus – see *RACKET-TAILED PARROTS*

Prosciger – see under *BLACK COCKATOOS*

PROTEIN, ANIMAL

Some parrot owners are at first aghast at the idea of feeding meat to their parrots, but the addition of animal protein to the diet helps to stimulate breeding in the larger parrots (such as macaws and Amazons) and, offered when chicks are being reared, helps to ensure that strong chicks are produced. Many parrot species are omnivorous in the wild and will consume animal protein.

Having noted the enthusiasm with which many parrots will eat cooked meat, this is totally credible. They relish chop bones and chicken carcases above all other food. Small, sharp bones should not be offered. Cooked lean meat left over from the table is recommended, and also filleted white fish, although fish is less popular than meat.

Hard-boiled egg is, of course, another excellent source of protein. To prevent waste, it can be minced. If fed cut into quarters, for example, most birds will pick out the yolk and leave the white.

The insect is the form of protein most commonly consumed by parrots in the wild. Some of these may be ingested accidentally, as insects on nectar, but there is no doubt that many species seek out insects, especially when rearing young. At least one species, the little Golden-winged Parrakeet (*Brotogeris chrysopterus*) regularly feeds on water snails; its longish narrow beak enabling it to remove them from the shells. The snails are stranded when the river level is low and are easily collected.

In captivity, many parrots appear to seek livefood when their chicks hatch. Australian parrakeets, such as Rosellas and *Barnardius* species, have been known to dig up earthworms and feed them to their young. One pair of Barnard's Parrakeets (*B. barnardius*) preferred chop bones to any other food when feeding chicks.

Mealworms will be consumed by many species of parrots when they have young, from small lorikeets, such as the Meyer's (*Trichoglossus flavoviridis meyeri*), to large ones such as cockatoos. One of the reasons cockatoos gnaw wood so avidly is in their search for beetles and their larvae. In captivity, however, mealworms are too stimulating to offer to these birds before chicks hatch – possibly resulting in the male attacking the female who is less advanced in breeding condition.

Cockatoos will also consume maggots when rearing young, however great care has to be exercised in feeding only maggots which have been cleaned for several days in bran. Any others are a possible source of botulism, a disease which kills countless wild birds and which has wiped out almost entire collections of captive birds. Some parrots also enjoy the chrysalids of maggots.

Livefood, such as mealworms or gentles, appears to be essential for breeding Hanging Parrots (*Loriculus*); chicks die at an early age if it is withheld. Ant pupae are also relished.

Greenfly and blackfly would appear to be very small fry for medium-sized parrots, yet a pair of Meyer's (*Poicephalus meyeri*) were observed gathering these from a privet hedge growing in their aviary.

Psephotus PARRAKEETS

This is a genus of extremes – it contains one of the parrakeets most popular with breeders and one which is shrouded in mystery – is it or is it not extinct? The Paradise Parrakeet (*P. pulcherrimus*) has been the subject of speculation for years. The interior of Australia is so vast that it is perfectly possible for a species to be unobserved by man for some years, as happened in the case of the Night Parrot. On the other hand, claims that this bird is in captivity are almost certainly fraudulent and perhaps the result of hybridising.

Two species of *Psephotus* are common in captivity, the Redrump (*P. haematonotus*) and the Many-coloured Parrakeet (*P. varius*), known as the Mulga Parrot in Australia. Sexual dimorphism is marked in all but one member of this genus. In the Redrump, the male is mainly green with the abdomen yellow and the rump red. The female is dull greyish-olive above and yellowish-olive below, with the rump green. The sexes can be distinguished in the nest, although a young male has less red on the rump than an adult.

There is an extremely popular yellow mutation in which the male is pale yellow, with the rump red, and the female is a pale creamy buff.

Redrumps are usually prolific, and thus their price is low. Four to six eggs are laid and incubated by the female for eighteen or nineteen days. The young spend about thirty days in the nest and their emergence is usually followed by the female producing a second clutch. This species is renowned for its capability as a foster parent and can be entrusted with the young of any Australian parrakeet.

These long-tailed parrakeets have a total length of 26–28 cm (10–11 in). Accommodation and feeding should be as recommended for *Barnardius*, but the length of the flight should be only 3.6 m (12 ft).

The Many-coloured male is a very colourful bird with a yellow forehead, red on the crown, yellow and orange on the abdomen and yellow on the shoulder and under tail coverts. The female is brownish on the head and upper breast and pale green below, with a little red ·on the shoulders. Immature birds are duller versions of the adults.

This species is a less prolific breeder; many chicks are lost because females cease to brood them at an early age. Chicks should therefore be checked first thing in the morning and again during the day, and removed for fostering or hand-rearing if necessary.

Both species have very pleasant voices and can be highly recommended as aviary birds. The other three *Psephotus*, the Hooded (*P. chrysopterygius dissimilis*), the Golden-shouldered (*P. c. chrysopterygius*) and the Blue-bonnet (*P. haematogaster*), are more difficult to breed and command much higher prices. They are recommended only for the experienced breeder.

Pseudeos LORY

The Dusky Lory (*P. fuscata*) is the only member of the genus. Its appearance and behaviour are distinctive. The coloration is highly unusual, being a blend of brilliant and subtle colours. There are two colour phases. In the more common one, the underparts are fiery orange and black, there is orange in the wings and the head and nape are orange, brown and black. In the other colour phase, the orange areas are replaced by yellow.

In both phases the upperparts are dark brown with copper and blue reflections, the under tail coverts are dark blue and the tail is bronze, blue and orange (or yellow). The beak and skin at the side of the lower mandible are orange, and the iris of the eye is brilliant orange. It is difficult to understand how the bird received its name – unless from an immature specimen – most young birds have very subdued coloration.

In length it is about 24 cm (9½ in). The rump colour varies – this is a sexual distinction in my experience, the rump colour of the male being yellow and white, while in the female the colour is more silvery.

The diet consists of nectar, fruit, spray millet and corn on the cob or sweet corn kernels. Bread and milk, or just milk, will be taken by some pairs when rearing young. A little sprouted sunflower seed can be offered after the chicks are about three weeks old.

The personality of the Dusky is extrovert. Fearless and noisy, some males become very aggressive when breeding. Duskies are generally seasonal rather than continuous nesters like so many lories. Two eggs are laid and incubated for twenty-four days by the female. The young spend eleven to twelve weeks in the nest. A nest-box for this species should measure about 23 cm (9 in) square and 61 cm (2 ft) high. Nest litter should be changed at least once every week when chicks are in the nest.

Dusky Lories are fanatical bathers; they are also very hardy and will bathe during very cold weather. My pair used to enjoy playing in snow! In the wild they occur at altitudes as high as 2,000 m (6,560 ft). Very widely distributed throughout New Guinea, they are found in groups or quite large flocks. The flight is extremely swift and either direct or swooping. At Loro Parque in Tenerife, the Dusky Lory is the most spectacular liberty bird. A small group delights in passing among a crowd of visitors at immense speed and so close they may brush past the people's ears. The speed and accuracy of their flight, often swooping and swerving just above ground level, is a joy to watch. First to rise and last to go to roost, the sky may be completely dark when the last bird reaches its roosting tree. They will follow the keeper operating the electric cart carrying the food to the parrots, and can often be seen perched on the cart helping themselves!

Those that are released adapt immediately to a life at liberty, moving around in search of flowering blossoms just as they would in the wild. In a suitable locality, no species can be more highly recommended as a liberty bird. It must be remembered, however, that the release of exotic birds is illegal in many areas.

Psittacella PARROTS
These birds are virtually unknown in aviculture and seldom observed in the wild because they are small, live in dense forest and have plumage which provides excellent camouflage. Mountain birds, they are found in New Guinea from about 1,700 m (5,600 ft) to apparently as high as 4,000 m (12,000 ft). Few other parrots have been found at such a high altitude. They eat seeds, berries and fruit.

Of the four species, probably only one has been kept in captivity. This is Brehm's Parrot (*P. brehmii*), the largest of the genus at 24 cm (9 in). (The smallest are only 14 cm/6 in.) All are barred with black and yellow on the mantle, rump and upper tail coverts, and also on the breast in some cases, and all have the under tail coverts red. They are sexually dimorphic, the female lacking the yellow band on the nape, but having the breast and/or flanks and side of the abdomen barred with black and yellow.

The members of this genus are likely to remain forever mysterious birds about which next to nothing is known.

PSITTACINE BEAK AND FEATHER DISEASE SYNDROME (PB AND FDS)
This is a viral disease which attacks the immune system, causing loss of feathers and abnormalities of the beak, and makes the victim vulnerable to all kinds of further infection. In fact, it could be compared with AIDS in human beings. It is possible that more than one kind of virus is involved, as the disease does not follow exactly the same pattern in all species.

Cockatoos are the most likely to be affected and in these birds the disease is usually evident at the first moult. Prior to this, the bird appears to be in perfect condition. However, the new feathers may remain in the quill which also contains blood, or those that erupt will be deformed and soon break off.

The plumage becomes progressively worse, no powder down is produced and, possibly within a couple of years, the bird is almost naked. The beak and nails become soft and overgrown and viral warts may appear on the feet. Alternatively, the beak may be unaffected. Some birds retain enough down to protect them from cold; others will need a heat lamp because they will be unable to maintain normal body temperature – although ensuring that plenty of food is always before them will help.

Some birds with this unfortunate disease become very depressed; in others morale and appetite are unaffected. A treatment that can slow down the pace of the disease has been developed. An autogenous vaccine is prepared using feather biopsies and beak scrapings. Weekly shots of the vaccine are given. However, only a

A Greater Vasa Parrot (*Coracopsis vasa vasa*), one year after losing all her feathers through psittacine beak and feather disease.

few veterinarians in the USA, and perhaps only one in the UK, have been prepared to do this to date. It must be emphasised that thus far no cure has been found – only a method of slowing down the progress of the disease. Affected birds can live for several years.

My experience with this disease relates to two Greater Vasa Parrots (*Coracopsis vasa*) which had a few white feathers in their plumage when obtained. After about a year, the amount of white feathers increased greatly and feather loss commenced. After another year the male was almost naked, but for a good covering of down, and the female possessed a few wisps of down and two or three primaries. These primaries were removed and examined under an electron microscope. It was found that a virus was present. In both birds beak and nails were normal, but the female had viral warts on her cere. When I moved from England to Tenerife, she was totally naked and had to be protected on the journey by placing the sleeve of a jumper over her body, with part of a pair of tights placed over this to keep it in place. She travelled well, but suffered a little bruising.

Vasas are fanatical sun-bathers and the warmth of Tenerife was much to the liking of the two affected birds. The female, now totally naked, will bathe with enthusiasm as soon as she is placed outdoors in the sun. The appetite and morale of both birds, one year after the move, seemed totally unaffected.

What to do with parrots affected with PB and FDS can be a dilemma. Not everyone would wish to care for such birds, or perhaps have the facilities (constant warmth) to do so. In that case they could donate them to an institution or veterinarian who is researching the disease, give them to someone who is prepared to care for them, or, as a last resort, have them humanely euthanised.

Psittacosis – see *ZOONOSES*

Psittacula Parrakeets
Long, or very long slender tails characterise the *Psittacula* parrakeets from Asia. In aviculture the members of this genus range from the very well known to the extreme rarity, from 30 cm (12 in) to 60 cm (2 ft), and from possessing the most subtle tones (as in the Plum-head) to the strong contrasts of the Derbyan. They are all sexually dimorphic.

Unsuitable as pets, they are extremely attractive aviary birds. Accommodation requirements vary from an aviary of 2.4 or 3 m (8 to 10 ft) for the smaller members of the genus, and also for the Ringneck, to a minimum of 3.6 m (12 ft) for Derbyans and Alexandrines. To appreciate their beauty in flight, the latter need an aviary length of 6 m (20 ft).

A female Derbyan Parrakeet, distinguished from the male by her black upper mandible and pink neck ring.

Feeding is simple, yet varied. They require a seed mixture (sunflower, canary, oats, white millet, buckwheat, a little hemp, peanuts, and for the larger species, pinenuts) and also spray millet. The usual fruits and berries will be enjoyed, as well as greenfood (spinach, sowthistle, chickweed, seeding grasses, dandelion, etc.). A nutritious rearing food is essential when chicks hatch, especially when there are as many as four or five.

Many *Psittaculas* are early nesters, especially Ringnecks and Plum-heads, laying in February or March. Derbyans tend to nest later. The clutch size averages four but can be up to six. Incubation is carried out by the female alone for twenty-three days in the Ringneck, and up to twenty-eight days in the Alexandrine. The young spend about seven weeks in the nest.

The seven best known *Psittaculas* are the Alexandrine, the Indian

Rosellas

The Mealy Rosella *(Platycercus adscitus palliceps)* is one of the most distinctively coloured of the Rosellas.

Brown's Rosella *(Platycercus venustus)* is the most expensive of the Rosellas.

The Stanley Parrakeet, or Western Rosella *(Platycercus icterotis icterotis)* is one of the most popular a free-breeding of th Rosellas. A female seen here.

Vasas

The Greater Vasa *(Coracopsis vasa vasa)* from Madagascar is probably one of the most primitive of parrots.

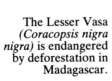

The Lesser Vasa *(Coracopsis nigra nigra)* is endangered by deforestation in Madagascar.

Ringneck, the African Ringneck, the Slaty-headed, the Long-tailed, the Moustached and the Derbyan.

Psittaculirostris – see under *FIG PARROTS*

Psittacus erithacus – see *GREY PARROT*

Psittinus PARROT

The single member of the genus, the Blue-rumped Parrot (*P. cyanurus*) is a most unusual and distinctive little bird. It reminds me of a miniature *Tanygnathus* in some respects, and also of the genus *Psittacula*. Only 18 cm (7½ in) in length, it is a quiet, rather inactive bird, which must be difficult to observe in the wild. It is found in Borneo, Sumatra, Thailand and the Malay Peninsula. Its status varies from common to rare, but it is widespread throughout the Malay Peninsula, including Singapore.

Although it has been exported fairly often, it has generally not proved easy to establish. In spite of its slightly hunched, top-heavy appearance, birds in good feather are extremely attractive. Above all, the voice is unlike that of any other parrot and decidedly pleasant to my ears. It makes a high-pitched piping sound.

Sexual dimorphism is pronounced in this little parrot. The male has a blue head and a red beak, whereas in the female the head is brown and the beak is black. In immature birds the head is green and the beak horn-coloured.

The plumage is otherwise mainly green and the feathers of the wing coverts are conspicuously margined with yellow, as in some *Tanygnathus* parrots. The prominent white iris of the eye gives the bird a rather mean appearance. In actual fact, this is quite appropriate where the female is concerned. As in some *Psittacula* species, she is dominant for most of the year and the male may be afraid of her.

The beak tends to become overgrown in some birds unless fresh wood for gnawing is regularly available. A wide variety of foods should be offered – all the small seeds, sunflower, various fruits, elderberries, rosehips, hawthorn berries, chickweed and other greenfood, small pine nuts and peanuts.

This species has bred in captivity, but only rarely. Three to five eggs are laid.

Psittrichas fulgidus – see *PESQUET'S PARROT*

PURPLE-BELLIED PARROT
(*Triclaria malachitacea*)

The single member of this genus is notable for its thrush-like song: the female also sings, but not quite so expressively. A beautiful bird with large dark eyes, it is one of my greatest favourites. Alas, it is rare and difficult to establish in captivity. Originating from south-eastern Brazil, it inhabits rainforest and woodland. There is no evidence that it is rare.

Sexual dimorphism in this species is pronounced. The male has a large patch of violet on his abdomen, being otherwise a rich and glossy dark green. The female lacks the violet patch. In length it is about 30 cm (12 in) including the tail which is long and quite broad.

Captive breeding, however, has rarely been achieved. Single youngsters were reared at Loro Parque, Tenerife, in 1985 and 1988.

Purple-bellied Parrots in my own collection were fed on sunflower seed, canary, niger, peanuts, pine nuts, a small piece of spray millet daily, various fruits, the berries of hawthorn and elder, and corn on

The Blue-rumped Parrot (this one is a male) is uncommon in captivity.

the cob. This species relishes the leaves and bark of freshly cut branches.

The clutch size is three or four and the incubation period appears to be twenty-eight days – a long period for a small parrot.

Purpureicephalus – see
PILEATED PARRAKEET

PYGMY PARROTS (*Micropsitta*)
The smallest parrots in existence, Pygmy Parrots measure only 8.5–10 cm (3½–4 in). The six species are unknown in captivity because they have proved impossible to keep alive. They are known to feed on small seeds, lichen, insects and fruits – but the few which have been captured refused to feed.

Their country of origin is New Guinea, and they are also found on the Solomon Islands. Their long toes, curved nails and stiffened tail feathers are adaptations for climbing up and down the trunks of trees in their search for food.

These tiny parrots are mainly green with contrasting colours on the head and breast.

Pyrrhura **CONURES**
Conures are not always appreciated because of their loud voices, but the *Pyrrhura* species are different. Their voices are quieter and their plumage is intricate and in most forms extremely attractive, as is their personality. They are intensely inquisitive birds and many become tame or fearless even although kept in an aviary. Ideal for breeders who do not have a lot of space, they will produce young in suspended cages 2 m (6 ft) long.

These conures originate from South and Central America. In all species plumage is alike in male and female. Their size ranges from 24 cm (9½ in) in *rupicola* to 28 cm (11 in) in the Blue-throated (*P. cruentata*). The latter differs from all the popularly kept members of the genus in not having the feathers of the throat and upper breast (or the nape in some species) margined with white or buff.

The diet should be as recommended for *Pionus*, omitting the walnuts and pine nuts. This is an ideal group for the specialist, who could commence with the free-breeding Red-bellied (*P. frontalis*) and Green-cheeked Conures (*P. molinae*) and progress to some of those which are less well established in captivity and, in the case of the Pearly (*Pyrrhura perlata lepida*) and the White-eared (*P. leucotis*), are endangered because of deforestation. There are sixteen species, nine of which are fairly well known in aviculture.

Some pairs prove very prolific. The clutch size varies with the species, being four to six in most, or eight to ten in the White-eared, Painted (*P. picta*) and the Rock Conure (*P. rupicola*). The incubation period is twenty-two to twenty-four days and the young remain in the nest for seven to eight weeks. The personality of hand-reared birds varies: *molinae* and *cruentata* can be nippy and unpleasant and decidedly aggressive towards other young birds, while others (including a *rupicola*) are enchantingly tame and affectionate.

The Red-bellied and the Green-cheeked differ little in plumage – and more than one sub-species of both are known in captivity, adding to the confusion of identification. However, the former has a narrow dark red frontal band, whereas in the Green-cheeked the forehead and the top of the head are brown, as is part of the ear coverts. The Red-bellied originates from south-eastern Brazil, Uruguay, north-eastern Argentina and eastern Paraguay, whereas the Green-cheeked is found in the Mato Grosso region of Brazil, and also in Bolivia and north-western Argentina. Both species are common in the wild.

Occasionally imported are the Black-tailed or Maroon-tailed Conures (*P. melanura*) from north-western South America, and the Painted Conure of the Amazon basin and Guyana. (Imported birds come from the latter country.)

Pesquet's Parrot
(Psittrichas fulgidus)
from New Guinea –
the only large parrot
which never eats
seed.

A miscellany of parrots (1)

Mexican Thick-billed Parrots *(Rhynchopsitta pachyryncha)* are endangered by the destruction of pine forests.

A male Blue-crowned Hanging Parrot *(Loriculus galgulus)* one of the most exquisite of small parrots.

The Black-headed Caique *(Pionites melanocephala melanocephala)* is found north of the Amazon, in the Guianas, Brazil and Venezuela.

The Brown-headed Parrot *(Poicephalus cryptoxanthus)* is the dullest-coloured of the genus, but young birds make most attractive pets.

Q

QUAKER PARRAKEET
(*Myiopsitta monachus*)

The Quaker is well known for two characteristics: its ability to colonise countries outside its native continent, and for the fact that it builds a large colonial nest of sticks. Sometimes called the Monk Parrakeet, its plumage is mainly grey and green, and its bill is brownish with a rounded appearance to the upper mandible. The cheeks and throat are grey, merging into the pale grey breast feathers which are tipped with white. Primary wing feathers are blue and black. In length it is about 29 cm (11½ in) including the longish tail.

This parrakeet occurs naturally in south-eastern South America (Argentina, Paraguay, Uruguay, Bolivia and Brazil). However, feral populations have become established in parts of the USA and in Europe. These are derived from escaped cage birds or those which have been deliberately released by a birdkeeper who enjoys watching several pairs at liberty on his property. They are so free-breeding that in some areas large populations have resulted after a few years.

They can be a menace to farmers because of their fondness for fruit and grain crops, otherwise it is a pleasure to watch them carrying sticks, building their nests and fledging their young. This unusual nest building habit arises from the fact that some areas of open Pampa, where they occur naturally, have no trees large enough to produce nesting holes.

In many areas, this is the most numerous and conspicuous member of the parrot family.

They can be offered a wide variety of seeds, fruits and vegetables, and also bread and milk and table scraps. Hand-reared birds make attractive pets and may learn to mimic. A colony aviary of Quakers is a never-ending source of interest, the only disadvantage being the continuous chattering and harsh calls which emerge from it.

At Loro Parque, in Tenerife, Quakers abound. They build their bulky nests in palm trees. A nest which fell from a palm onto my terrace contained six chambers, plus two sparrows' nests. There is no lining, and the eggs are laid on the carefully woven twigs. They commence to nest in March. Five or six eggs are laid, but three or four seem to be the usual number of young to emerge at the end of May.

Some pairs breed again and more young will be in evidence in September. Inevitably a number leave the nest prematurely and quickly find homes with the local people, who will hand-rear them as pets. First, however, they have to be bathed, for they are generally crawling with red mites. Young birds are easily distinguished by their shorter tails, whiter skin surrounding the eye, generally more docile appearance and bolder behaviour.

Quakers are ideal beginner's birds, being very easy to feed, hardy and willing to breed. In an aviary they will use a nest-box, or construct a stick nest if given a wire base and a large supply of sticks. Nest inspection is almost impossible because a short tunnel leads to the nest chamber.

There is a rare and expensive blue mutation and an even rarer, and more expensive, beautiful yellow mutation of the Quaker Parrakeet.

A Quaker Parrakeet (*Myiopsitta monachus*) at its nest constructed from twigs.

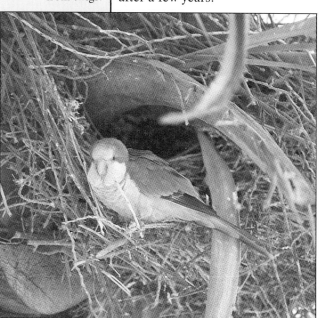

R

RACKET-TAILED PARROTS
(*Prioniturus*)

These parrots are so called because of their two elongated tail feathers, each of which has a spatule or racket at the tip. The shaft of the feather is bare. The racket-bearing feathers extend for 65–90 mm (2½–3½ in) beyond the length of the other tail feathers in the male and are shorter in the female. It takes six weeks for one of these feathers to grow, after which the other one will be moulted and replaced.

Racket-tails, of which there are six species, are found in Indonesia and the Philippines. They measure 27–32 cm (11–12 in), one species, *flavicans*, being 37 cm (14 in). Sexual dimorphism can be pronounced or slight, and coloration is pleasing – shades of green, with soft, contrasting colours on head or nape.

Members of this genus are rare in captivity, mainly because they are difficult to establish. Most of the few exported die within a few weeks or months of capture. I know of only one bird which has survived for a number of years. A Blue-crowned (*P. discursus*), it was kept as a pet for at least twelve years by the late Fred Keen of Middlesex, England. It took three years to persuade it to eat anything other than cooked rice and raw egg. It eventually acquired a taste for cheese, the pips of pears and crusts of bread.

If the opportunity occurs to keep Racket-tails, they should be offered plenty of fruit, the usual seeds, corn on the cob, boiled maize, peanuts, carrot and bread and milk.

One of the most beautiful of the Racket-tails is the Golden-mantled (*P. platurus*). The soft green of the male's plumage is enhanced by small areas of pastel colours – pink on the crown, bordered by a patch of lavender grey, dull gold on the mantle and lilac on the shoulders. The female is entirely green, and lighter below. Young birds resemble the female except for the central tail feathers, which lack the rackets, but have pointed tips.

This species is very rare in aviculture. However, in December 1987, I saw it amid unforgettable surroundings. Miami Metrozoo has undoubtedly one of the world's finest aviaries, called 'Wings of Asia'. Within its 6,100 sq m (1½ acres), it reproduces various Asian habitats – rainforest, swamp, etc. The spacious and natural surroundings enable the occupants to behave exactly as they would in the wild. Curator Ron Johnson told me that there was a male Golden-mantled Racket-tail within, but that we would be unlikely to see it as it was shy.

Eventually, a strange, almost unparrot-like call alerted us to its presence high in a tree. Then it flew down lower and perched amid surroundings so perfect I could imagine I was observing it on an Indonesian island.

Off-exhibit, yet within the confines of the aviary, another pair of Racket-tails are housed and this male often visits the vicinity of their cage. If they breed, I believe they will be the first Racket-tails to do so in captivity.

RED MITES (*Dermanyssus* species)

Red mites are perhaps the most harmful and debilitating of all lice and mites which attack cage birds. Unlike featherlice, for example, red mites do not live permanently on the bird, but in cracks in the cage, nest-box or enclosure. They emerge at night to feed on the blood of birds, possibly causing anaemia or the death of the chicks.

In a severe case, both nest and chicks could be swarming with red mites: in the dark environment of the nest the mites can live permanently on the chicks. If such a case is discovered, the chicks must be treated instantly, if feathered, by dipping them in an insecticide formulated for birds. Obviously the eggs should not be immersed in insecticide. On no account should they be returned to the nest-box, which must be burnt or properly sterilised. A new nest-box must be used and a watch kept for any recurrence of the mites.

Breeders must be ever on the alert for signs of these mites: clusters of grey particles on woodwork or other surfaces are

A miscellany of parrots (2)

The Blue-rumped Parrot *(Psittinus cyanurus)* is not well known in captivity. It is quiet in voice and personality. The head is blue in the male and brown in the female.

Above: Desmarest's Fig Parrot is typical of the genus of beautiful *Psittaculirostris* Fig Parrots from New Guinea.

Male and female Ecletus Parrots (*Eclectus roratus vosmaeri*). The female is distinguished from other sub-species by her yellow under tail coverts.

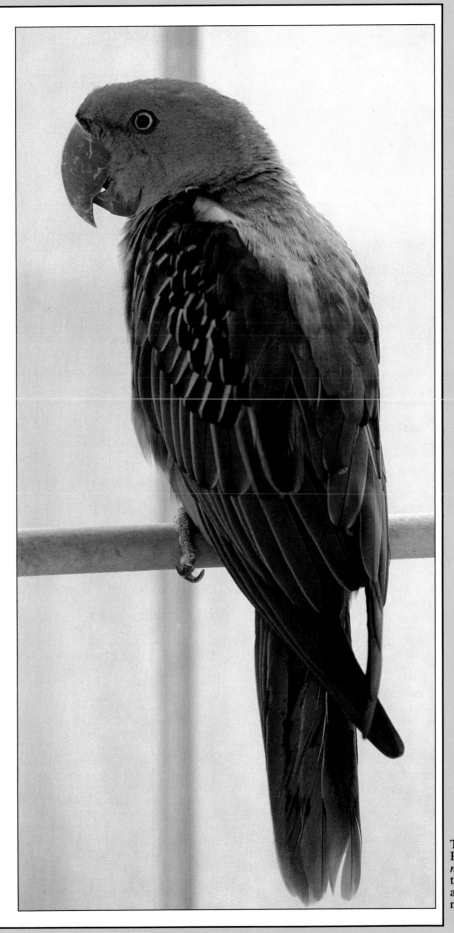

The Great-billed
Parrot *(Tanygnathus
megalorynchos)* has
the most beautiful
and intricate wing
markings.

their faeces. The mites themselves can be seen with the naked eye, and appear red after having fed on blood. Adult birds must be treated with a proprietary powder formulated to rid birds of lice and mites. This can be obtained from pet stores and suppliers. Pyrethrum is a good deterrent.

After treating or painting woodwork in cages or a birdroom, many dead mites may be found, and this can be the first indication many breeders have that these mites are present. The use of a dichlorvos strip in a birdroom will kill them – however, care must be taken that the strip is the correct size for the room, or area, or it could have a harmful effect on small birds.

Rhynchopsitta PARROTS

The feathered face and shorter tail distract one's attention from the otherwise macaw-like features of the Thick-billed Parrot (*R. pachyrhyncha*) and the Maroon-fronted Parrot (*R. terrisi*). Some taxonomists regard them as sub-species rather than as separate species. They measure 38 cm (15 in) and 43 cm (17 in) respectively.

The Thick-billed Parrot is a most attractive shade of dark green. Its forehead and crown are red, and it also has a broad red stripe through the eye. The bend and edge of the wing and the thighs are also dark red. The underwing coverts are bright yellow. Immature birds have much less red in the plumage, this being mainly on forehead and forecrown. The skin surrounding the eye is whitish (yellow in adults).

This species has the most northerly distribution of any neotropical parrot. It formerly occured in the southern states of the USA, in southern Arizona and New Mexico, being an irregular winter visitor there until about 1930. It is not known whether it ever bred in the USA or was a visitor in times of food shortages only. More recently it has been found only in Mexico, but has nested within 150 km (93 miles) of the US border. If it could be re-established in the USA, this could ultimately prove crucial for its conservation, in view of the loss of its habitat and, particularly, the larger pine trees or snags (dead stumps) in which it nests.

Formerly the mountains of Arizona were the scene of ranching, mining and prospecting; many men had guns and many Thick-bills must have been shot. Now the human population there is very much smaller and the habitat is excellent, with many potential nest sites in old woodpecker holes. Little timber-felling has occurred as the steep slopes make this difficult.

The large influx of Thick-bills smuggled into the USA in 1985 and 1986 (estimates vary from several hundred to over one thousand) produced the idea of re-establishing this species in Arizona. In September 1986, the first release of thirteen confiscated, wild-caught birds was made. On 16 October more were released. The resulting high mortality among these birds could have been avoided: releases coincided with the autumn migration of raptors who were more than a match for the less than perfect flight ability of some of the Thick-bills. Future releases will, it is hoped, be made with more care and this handsome parrot will again be counted as a native bird of the USA.

The Thick-bill is being bred in few collections; most private aviculturists consider it too noisy and destructive. However, outside the USA very few Thick-bills have been available and, at the time of writing, there was much controversy as to whether aviculturists in the USA would be permitted to keep these parrots because they are a native species.

The clutch size is two to four eggs and the incubation period is twenty-six days. In Europe this species nests late in the year (August or September) and has not proved prolific.

The Maroon-fronted Parrot differs from the Thick-bill in having the forehead maroon-brown, as the name suggests. The bend and edge of the wings and the thighs are brownish-red and the under wing coverts are silver-grey. It occurs only in north-eastern Mexico, being found in pine forests, usually at an elevation of 2,000 to 3,500 m (6,560–11,500 ft).

Its population has decreased considerably in recent years, as its limited nesting area makes it a highly vulnerable species. The nest sites are holes in cliffs. Ravens have been seen entering known parrot nesting holes and are therefore almost certainly taking eggs or chicks. Also, the mixed conifer forests, on which Maroon-Fronted Parrots depend for food, are being destroyed by fire, logging, grazing and clearing.

This species is unknown in captivity.

RINGING (BANDING)

Closed rings (seamless bands) are becoming of increasing importance in parrot aviculture. They are the only positive evidence that a bird has been bred in captivity. Much present-day legislation requires such evidence. A closed ring can only be placed on the leg of a parrot chick during the first few days or weeks (depending on the species) of its life. If it is of the correct size, it can be removed only by cutting with pliers. If it is too large, it can still be removed when the bird is almost adult size.

Many breeders are reluctant to ring chicks because a ring can present a lethal hazard, and cause serious leg injury, or even the loss of the leg. The problem is that very little has been published about the correct ring sizes for the many different species bred in captivity. If the ring is too tight, the leg will become swollen. If this is not noticed, the result may be loss of the blood supply to the leg. Or dirt could lodge under the ring, causing an infection which also necessitates immediate removal of the ring.

If the ring used (normally made of metal) is not sufficiently strong for the species, there is a danger that the bird could crush it out of shape so that it digs into the leg. If it is too wide, a callous will result. In choosing a ring, one must therefore take into account the circumference of the tarsus, the length of the tarsus from the hind toes, and the strength of the bill of the species concerned. The length of the bird is absolutely no indication of the correct ring size. Lories, for example, have much thicker legs than Australian parrakeets of the same size.

Small parrakeets (thin legs) can be ringed at an early age, about eight or ten days, whereas larger birds with thick legs cannot be ringed until they are about four weeks old in some instances. The age will vary in the same species;

not only is there individual variation, but hand-reared birds will generally be ringed later than those which are parent-reared, because their initial growth is slower.

If a chick is ringed too early, or the ring is too large, it will come off, not necessarily on the day following ringing, but up to several days later. If I believe I have ringed a chick too early, but know I will not be able to check the nest the following day, I push the ring up onto the tibia, and move it down onto the tarsus a few days later. The ring is normally placed on the tarsus, but in actual fact it does not matter if it stays on the tibia.

The best instrument for ringing small and medium-sized parrots is a wooden toothpick; alternatively, a sharpened matchstick can be

used. The ring is pushed over the three largest toes and the smallest one is then released with the aid of the toothpick. With large chicks, like cockatoos and macaws, the ring is best pushed over all four toes, over the tarsus and up onto the tibia. If left too late, it can be very hard to release the toe of a large chick. In a difficult case, put a little petroleum jelly over the toes to ease the passage of the ring.

With some aviary birds, ringing is a hazard because the parents object to the ring and eject the chick from the nest in trying to remove it. In hole-nesting birds, where the interior of the nest is dark, this is not normally a problem. *Forpus* parrotlets, however, often try to remove rings. In one nest, a pair of *conspicillatus* were breeding for the first time

Closed rings of various diameters and thicknesses. Those above the toothpick are 14-mm (½ in) and 18 mm (¾ in), suitable for macaws and cockatoos. The toothpick is used for putting the smaller rings on chicks' legs.

Bronze-winged
Pionus *(Pionus
chalcopterus)* – an
unusually coloured
parrot which is not
often imported.

A miscellany of parrots (3)

The female Purple-bellied Parrot *(Triclaria malachitacea)* is easily distinguished from the male: she lacks the purple on her breast.

Male Red-capped Parrot *(Pionopsitta pileata)*.

The Short-tailed Parrot *(Graydidascalus brachyurus)* is reminiscent of a miniature Amazon Parrot.

Highly intelligent and mischievous, the Kea *(Nestor notabilis)* is a mountain parrot from New Zealand.

No problems are encountered in ringing most parrot chicks in the nest. *Forpus* parrotlets are an exception. Two of the four Spectacled chicks seen here had their legs mutilated by their parents after ringing. One lost a leg as a result.

when the three eldest chicks were ringed. The parents broke the leg of one chick and so badly mutiliated the leg of another that the leg was lost.

Rings are frequently a danger in an aviary also, where the bird may become caught on a projecting piece of wire or even on a natural perch. I would urge all breeders to examine the interior of a cage or aviary with great care before placing a ringed bird inside. Also, when constructing cages from welded mesh, never turn back the mesh around the edges of doors, for example; always cut the wire off, leaving as little projecting as possible.

Technology is improving in the manufacture of rings, and the designs will surely become more sophisticated. A German manufacturer is now producing a smooth, extremely strong, plastic ring with no straight edges. Numbers and letters, which can easily be read through the plastic, are printed inside, the information required being given when the rings are ordered.

Breeders must ring their chicks. Within a few years it is likely to be compulsory for the export of all parrots and for the sale of endangered species. Already the implementation of CITES is different for captive-bred birds. Closed rings are still the most effective way of identifying individual birds. This is of vital importance where the rarer species are concerned, to prevent related birds being paired together.

All ring numbers must be recorded in an easily accessible manner – either notebook or computer. Perhaps the day will come when there is a central registry and the information recorded on a ring will be intelligible to all with a code book, as is presently the case with the UK Budgerigar Society, for example.

RODENT CONTROL

Aviaries, and the plentiful supply of food they contain, invariably attract mice, rats and other vermin. Only enclosures with concrete floors, 9-mm (³⁄₈-in) welded mesh and no gaps anywhere in the construction are rodent-proof – so very few are free from these pests. They consume and contaminate food, carry disease and disturb and even kill the occupants and their young in the nest.

Every effort must be made to keep their numbers under control or losses will be heavy. Poison or traps must be placed in boxes which birds cannot enter; however, it is pointless putting out poison unless all food is removed from the aviary every night. This is a time-consuming task which may not be possible in many instances, but little success will be achieved in controlling rodents unless it is carried out.

A successful and humane type of mouse trap is a box with a special flap through which it is easily entered; once inside, however, the mouse cannot escape. Any number can be caught in one night. Those who dislike killing any form of life can then release the occupants – preferably several miles away, as mice seem to have a good homing sense! These traps are marketed commercially.

ROSELLAS (*Platycercus*)

Few genera of parrots are more popular with breeders than the Rosellas. Brightly coloured parrakeets from Australia, they are hardy and easy to care for and most are very free-breeding. They tend to be aggressive, so the strict rule is one pair per aviary. There should be double wiring between adjoining enclosures and, where possible, pairs of Rosellas should not be housed next door to each other.

These parrakeets are recognised by the distinctive pattern of the feathers of the mantle and part of the wing coverts; these feathers are black in the centre and yellow or red on the margin, according to the species. The length varies from 25 cm (10 in) in the Stanley, to 36 cm (14 in) in the Green (*P. caledonicus*) and the Pennants, including, of course, the long broad tail.

Rosellas do best in outdoor aviaries which are at least 4 m (13 ft) long. A seed mixture forms a large part of the diet and should consist of canary, oats, buckwheat, wheat, sunflower seed and a little hemp in winter. Spray millet is relished, as is greenfood which should be offered daily and greatly increased when chicks hatch. The larger species will eat small pine nuts and also peanuts.

During the rearing period a more nutritious food, such as bread and milk, or a proprietary rearing food, is essential for good results. Rosellas seek a source of protein then, even consuming earthworms from the aviary floor. Apple, and occasionally other fruit, carrot and berries are also eaten.

Sexing Rosellas can be difficult; generally speaking, males have a broader head and larger bill and are more brightly coloured. Care must be taken in introducing the male into the female's aviary (never vice versa); if he behaves aggressively it may be necessary to clip his wings.

The breeding life of these parrakeets can be very long – up to twenty years and commencing at one or two. Nest-boxes should measure about 23 cm (9 in) square and be at least 60 cm (2 ft) high. The incubation period is about twenty days and the young spend five weeks in the nest. Clutch size varies from five to ten, according to species.

The most popular and inexpensive species is the Red Rosella (*P. eximius*) usually called the Golden-mantled, although this name should refer only to the sub-species *cecilae*, which has richer yellow on the margins of the feathers of the upper parts, and a greenish-blue rump – not pale green as in the nominate race. Both have a red head and upper breast, white cheeks and yellow abdomen – very colourful birds.

This is rivalled by the beautiful Pennant's Parrakeet (*P. elegans elegans*), known as the Crimson Rosella in Australia. The cheeks, tail and part of the wings are blue, the centres of the feathers of the back are black and the rest of the plumage is crimson. The smallest of the genus is the Stanley, or Western Rosella (*P. icterotis*), a very popular bird, and sexually dimorphic. The cheeks are yellow, brighter in the male, his head and underparts are scarlet (patchy red and green in females and young birds) and the markings on the wings and back of both sexes are black, green and blue.

One of the rarest and most expensive species, originating from the subtropical part of northern Australia, is the Brown's, or Northern Rosella (*P. venustus*). It is not easy to breed, partly because it chooses to nest during the winter months, and because there are often compatibility problems between male and female. For this reason, pairs should be formed when the birds are young.

S

SECURITY
Unfortunately, thefts of parrots, usually from outdoor aviaries, are common. All aviaries should be padlocked, and proper fittings should be used for the padlocks, not those which can be easily wrenched off or unscrewed. A covered run can be built around the entire perimeter of the aviaries, where a guard dog can run night and day. An electronic alarm system is very useful if the premises are never unattended. In this case, build the aviaries in a straight line to reduce the number of sensors required, thereby lessening the cost. The system which relies on a single infra-red beam at each point is not recommended, because it will frequently be set off by cats and other animals. To prevent this, two beams should be situated, one above the other, so that only a human is likely to activate the alarm.

SEED
A mixture of seeds is an important part of the diet of most parrakeets, conures, lovebirds and cockatiels. It should be offered to large parrots – most Eclectus and even some Amazons prefer small seeds to sunflower. There is little point in offering a mixture which contains sunflower and a small amount of other seeds, as the small ones usually get lost and wasted in the bottom of the container. By offering them separately, one can control the amount and prevent wastage. If small seeds are uneaten they should be discontinued.

Seeds such as canary and millet are best bought separately so that they can be offered on their own or in mixtures, according to the preferences of individual birds. If this is not possible, and there is a lot of waste, throw the discarded seed into boxes of earth; when the seedlings grow, place them, still in the box, in the aviary. The growing shoots will be eagerly devoured by most species.

A breakdown of the content (for protein, etc.) of the various seeds could be misleading, as this can vary considerably according to the part of the world in which they have been grown, but generally speaking small seeds contain in the region of 15% protein. Sunflower and hemp have a high oil content (as do niger and linseed which are more often fed to canaries and finches, but which make a useful winter supplement for any small parrots which will eat them) and canary and millet have a high carbohydrate content, in the region of 50% or 60%.

The staple ingredients of most seed mixtures are canary and millet. Canary does not vary significantly, except in size but there are a number of kinds of millet. Panicum is recommended for lovebirds, *Neophemas*, Hanging Parrots and Fig Parrots and white millet for most parrakeets, including *Neophemas*, Eclectus and other large parrots which enjoy small seeds. Red millet is not used for cage birds. Spray millet is relished by almost all parrots, from lorikeets to macaws and cockatoos. Oats, groats, wheat and buckwheat can be used to add variety to the mixture. Safflower can be fed instead of, or as well as, sunflower.

SEED, SUNFLOWER
Many pet parrots are fed primarily on sunflower seed, either through ignorance or lack of perseverance on the part of the owner. Sunflower, in moderation, is an excellent food, as it is relatively high in protein and other energy-giving nutrients, but if fed in excessive quantities dietary deficiencies are liable to occur, notably of the minerals and vitamins which are found in fresh fruits and vegetables. Therefore, the sunflower content of any parrot's diet should not exceed 60%.

Several years ago, it was rumoured in the USA that sunflower contains papaverine which was said to be addictive. This is untrue. It was also believed to cause obesity, which was not borne out in an experiment carried out at the University of California in Davis (Department of Avian Sciences). In young cockatiels fed only on millet or canary seed for sixty days, the weight gains were greater than those fed only sunflower for the same period.

I believe that providing sunflower *ad lib* is harmful to the livers of small species, but know of countless large parrots, such as Greys and Amazons, who have lived for many years on a diet consisting mainly of sunflower.

This is certainly not to be recommended, but it quite often happens that someone buys or inherits a pet parrot (especially a Grey) which will eat no other seed than sunflower, which should

Sunflower seed.

therefore be offered sprouted. In this condition the vitamin content is increased many times; it is easier to digest and nutritionally far superior to dry sunflower.

I soak all sunflower seed before it is offered, partly to remove dirt and other impurities, and partly because it is more palatable after soaking. Simply soak in cold water for twenty-four hours, then rinse well before feeding.

The quality, as well as the cleanliness, of sunflower seed is very important. On buying a new batch of sunflower seed, it is advisable to test it for germination. If a seed does not sprout, it means that the germ is dead and the seed is of little nutritional value. About 90% or more of the seeds should germinate. I would consider 60% to be a low germination rate.

The price of sunflower varies considerably according to the type (white is more expensive as less is grown, but it is said to have a lower oil content). Seed which has been cleaned well is always more expensive. Cleanliness is of great importance. For those who do not normally soak seed, I would suggest that soaking is carried out initially to ascertain how much dirt the seed contains.

Striped sunflower is the kind most often fed to parrots. There are different types and the most obvious differences lie in the shape and size of the seed. Look for a plump seed with a plump kernel. A long seed with a slim kernel inside is not good value as the ratio of kernel to husk is low.

SELLING

Much advice is offered on buying birds, but the very important subject of selling is usually neglected. Birds are sold either through word of mouth or by placing an advertisement in an avicultural journal, or possibly a local newspaper. For security reasons, it is advisable to give a box or telephone number, but no address, in an advertisement. (In the USA it is common practice to give only a first name, so that an interested person is unable to obtain the address from a telephone directory. This is wise in the case of very valuable birds.) When describing birds in advertisements, state species (including scientific name in the case of something unusual), young or adult, sex if known and method of sexing (proved breeder, surgical or feather sexing).

Allow the purchaser to see the bird. Except in special circumstances, do not send off, by rail or air, birds which have not been seen before purchase. Instead, if possible, send a photograph of the bird or birds in advance, especially if of a rare species. Explain that the birds are sent at the purchaser's risk. Any physical defect, such as a missing toe, must be pointed out before purchase, and also the fact that this was taken into account when the price was calculated.

Worm Australian parrakeets, and other species which are very susceptible to worms, a few days before purchase. Never carry this out on the day of sale, as the combined stress of worming and moving the bird could cause its death. It might also cause it to vomit in the buyer's presence. Explain the worming procedure to novice buyers.

If the purchaser is travelling by car, ask him or her to bring a suitable cage or carrying box. Different species, unless closely related and small, should be placed in separate carrying boxes. Large parrots, even mated pairs, should not travel in the same cage or box, as the stress of close confinement might cause the male to attack the female.

The purchaser should be allowed to examine the bird in the hand.

Explain how the bird has been fed. Give the buyer enough of the basic diet to last one or two days, so that the bird is not faced with unfamiliar food as well as unfamiliar surroundings. If necessary, advise the buyer on suitable accommodation.

Establish whether the bird is being sold on approval, that is, whether you will allow its return and repay the money if there is a legitimate complaint. Some breeders will do this for the bird's sake, because they do not wish it to remain with someone who is not happy with it, or who may sell it on to someone unsuitable.

SEXING, FEATHER CHROMOSOME

All birds have a chromosomal mechanism by which their sex is determined. Male birds have two Z sex chromosomes (usually called X) and females have one Z and one W. The latter can be identified under a microscope. Marc Valentine, a young American, pioneered the method of sexing birds using a blood feather (one which is still growing and therefore has blood in the shaft), which is removed from the bird to be sexed. The pulp is removed from the feather shaft and a cell culture is grown from the pulp. All that is required is one blood quill (perhaps two in a small bird), which must be kept sterile and must reach the laboratory within twenty-four hours.

After seven to ten days, enough cells have grown in the culture to enable a chromosome preparation to be made. The chromosomes are then analysed, thus determining sex, and also whether the bird possesses any chromosomal defects. For example, some birds are genetically inter-sex (neither male nor female) and are therefore sterile. Outwardly normal, this could never be discovered in any other manner.

Using this method, birds of any age can be sexed. Young can now be sold as sexed pairs as soon as they are independent. This is one of the most important avicultural breakthroughs ever made. At present, the service is available only in the USA, but it will eventually become the most widely used method of sexing birds.

An interesting spin-off of Dr Valentine's work is that comparative cytogenetics can now be used to interpret evolutionary relationships of different groups of birds, or even, more rarely, those within one genus. Using the staining technique, known as C-banding, on seventeen species of Amazon Parrots, Dr Valentine discovered a commonly derived feature in Dufresne's, Festive and Mealy Amazons, which is not ancestral to the entire genus.

SEXING, SURGICAL

Surgical sexing (laparoscopy) is a service provided by many avian veterinarians in the USA and by relatively few elsewhere. The laparoscope is an instrument used in human medicine to provide an internal examination of various parts of the body. Used with a light source, it is an excellent means of examining birds internally, for diagnostic purposes as well as for determining sex. Species as small as lovebirds can be sexed with perfect safety, provided that a small-sized laparoscope is used.

So that the bird does not suffer, it is first anaesthetised. There are two methods, gas (usually isofluorane) or injection. Gas has the advantage that after the mask is held over a bird's face, it is unconscious in seconds and is sexed and on its feet again in five minutes (in skilful hands). The main disadvantage is that individual birds react differently to gas and the correct dosage may be difficult to determine. When this method is employed, the owner is usually asked to withhold food during the previous twelve hours –

or less for a small bird.

When the anaesthetic is injected, no food should be provided for the previous three or four hours. It may be several hours before the bird regains consciousness. During this period, it is wrapped in a towel which is lightly taped to keep it in place. When it frees itself it will be very unsteady on its feet for half an hour or so and should be kept in a warm room for the remainder of the day. The following day it can be returned to its aviary.

The sexing procedure is normally quite simple. Feathers are plucked from a small area behind the last rib on the left side. The area is cleaned with surgical spirit, a small incision is made and the laparoscope is inserted. A light source and transmitting cable illuminate the bird's internal organs to reveal ovaries or testes. A vet can observe whether these organs are active and whether they are abnormal in any way, and also whether the bird is immature. In addition, a good view can be obtained of the air sacs, lungs, liver and kidneys.

This should be a fool-proof method of sexing adult birds in good health. On occasions, sex is impossible to determine, however, usually because the bird is overweight, or possibly because of some abnormality. A competent vet will state if the sex is in doubt and make no charge.

Most mistakes are made with immature birds which are declared females when, in fact, they are young males. Some 'mistakes' may be due to the fact that the owner has confused the birds. Parrots should be identified by a sexing ring, or by a tattoo, at the time of sexing. At Loro Parque, for example, a black ring is placed on the male's right leg and a gold ring on the female's left leg at the time of sexing. The ring number is recorded at that time.

If the bird is not given some mark of identification at the time of sexing, the owner should examine it carefully for some distinguishing mark – perhaps a missing nail, enlarged nostril, different coloration of feet or cere, abnormally coloured feather which is replaced at each moult, etc. All owners should, in any case, keep a record card for each bird, with a photograph of the bird and a note of any distinguishing marks. This could provide the means of recovery if the bird is stolen.

After a bird has been sexed, it should be kept indoors for the remainder of the day. On no account should it be returned to an aviary containing other birds. It may not be fully recovered and will therefore be vulnerable to attack.

The slight element of risk involved in surgical sexing arises mainly from the use of the anaesthetic, not from the surgical procedure. Incidentally, some vets will close the incision with a single stitch; others do not.

SEXUAL DIMORPHISM

Sexual dimorphism means that the male and female of a species are different in appearance. In parrots the difference is usually in plumage coloration and, in a few species, in beak coloration. In other species of birds there are other differences, such as size, colour of feet and even shape of the beak.

Sexual dimorphism may be subtle or slight. It is subtle, for example, in some Rosella parrakeets (*Platycercus*) in which the male is a little more brightly coloured than the female, as in the Golden-mantled Rosella (*P. eximius*). It is so subtle in some species that it may not be recognised. In Grey Parrots (*Psittacus erithacus*), males from the same area are usually darker than females.

In some species of *Psittacula* parrakeets, beak colour *and* plumage are different in male and female (such as the Derbyan Parrakeet, *P. derbiana*), while in other members of the genus only the plumage differs. The male Ringneck (*P. krameri*) has a black and pink ring around the neck, whereas the female is all green (as are young birds).

The Eclectus Parrot is the most extreme example of sexual dimorphism among parrots; indeed, few more striking examples occur throughout the avian world. The male is bright green with red under the wings, whereas the female flaunts a wonderful colour scheme of red and mauve or red and blue – but mainly red.

None of the theories which have been advanced as to why sexual dimorphism exists are satisfactory where the Eclectus is concerned. In most sexually dimorphic parrots, immature birds resemble the female, but in Eclectus there is no immature phase of the plumage. They can be sexed as soon as the first contour feathers appear at the age of three and a half to four weeks. It is not surprising that male and female Eclectus were once believed to be different species.

A less striking example of male and female being sufficiently different to be mistaken for two species, occurs in a small number of the genus *Charmosyna*.

An unusual form of sexual dimorphism is that which occurs in one of the world's best-known cage birds, the budgerigar (*Melopsittacus undulatus*). The cere, the bare, rounded area of flesh surrounding each nostril, is blue in adult males and brown in adult females in breeding condition (pale blue or whitish blue in immature females or those out of breeding condition). In young males it is a pinkish mauve colour. The only budgerigars which are difficult to sex by cere colour are certain mutations, such as lutino, albino and some pieds.

Unfortunately for the breeder, most parrots are either not sexually dimorphic or the difference is so slight as not to be recognised, or to be considered an unreliable method of determining sex.

SHINING PARROTS (*Prosopeia*)
The largest and among the most striking of all parrakeets, the two members of this genus are extremely rare in captivity. They come from Fiji, where their export has been prohibited for many years. Deforestation is threatening their survival, as is the practice of removing all the larger trees in excess of 33 cm (13 in) in diameter, which means that, in some areas, few remain with cavities large enough to provide nesting sites for Shining Parrots. These birds are not yet rare, but loss of nesting sites can cause a sudden decline in a population, which is then impossible to reverse because there are too few young birds.

There are too few birds outside Fiji for captive breeding to aid their survival and, in any case, the *Prosopeia* parrots are not easy to breed. This is more likely to be achieved in a warm climate, because they are in breeding condition for only a short time, and

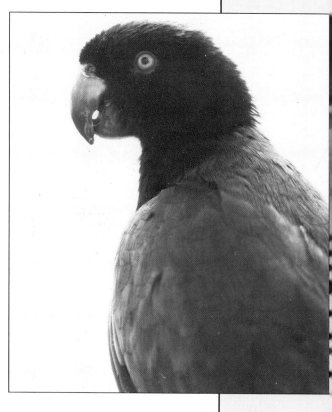

in Europe, for example, this is generally during cold weather.

One of the few European breeders found that the young were often killed, or died, within their first week.

One aspect of their care which does not present any difficulties is feeding. They accept an extremely wide variety of foods – virtually anything offered. Fruits, vegetables, seeds, nuts, meat (raw or cooked), mealworms and bread and milk are all eagerly consumed.

One to three eggs are laid and the incubation period is twenty-four days. The young spend about eight weeks in the nest. On hatching chicks have long silver-grey down, except for a patch of white down on the head, like *Eunymphicus* and *Cyanoramphus*.

The Masked Shining Parrot (*P. personata*) has very rarely been kept in captivity outside Fiji, where it is known only from the island of Viti Levu. It is mainly green with a black face, the centre of the breast and underparts yellow, and orange on the abdomen. The iris of the eye is a penetrating and vivid orange. The beak is grey-black in adults and paler in younger birds. In length it is 47 cm (19 in).

The Red Shining Parrot (*P.*

The Shining Parrot (*Prosopeia tabuensis*) – a rarely kept species from Fiji.

tabuensis) has several sub-species. *P. t. splendens* from Kandavu is distinctive because the head and underparts are crimson. There is a broad blue collar between nape and mantle. Wings and rump are bright green. The beak and iris of the eye are as described for *personata*. In length it is slightly smaller.

The other sub-species have maroon underparts and a narrow or wide blue band on the nape, or may lack this feature. A written description can do no justice to the beauty of these birds. Their long, broad tails, majestic bearing and peculiar, but smooth type of feather (in which each feather is not easily defined on the head, as in Eclectus) make them unique.

SHORT-TAILED PARROT
(*Graydidascalus brachyurus*)

The single member of this genus is distinctive, although somewhat reminiscent of a miniature Amazon (especially the Festive, which is found in the same area). It originates from the Amazon basin (Colombia, Ecuador, Peru and Brazil) and inhabits the flooded areas along the larger rivers. Quite common in the wild, it is very rare in captivity and captive breeding has yet to occur. The females of one aviculturist, who lacked males, laid clutches of one or two eggs. This species has a loud voice for its small size. Care and feeding should be as described for *Pionus* Parrots.

SPIX'S MACAW (*Cyanopsitta spixii*)

In appearance and behaviour, this species, the only member of its genus, is quite unlike other macaws. It is the only bird classified as a macaw that has its head entirely feathered, in this respect resembling the conures. The coloration is unique, being soft blue with the head pale greyish. In length it is 56 cm (22 in). The bill is black in adults and greyish-black with light markings in immature birds.

Known only from north-eastern Brazil, the remaining small population had virtually been trapped out of existence by 1987 when it was rumoured that the last three known birds had been caught. If another population exists, it is probably very small.

Thus, this must be considered the most endangered of all parrots from continental South America.

In 1988, the number of Spix's Macaws known in captivity (none were known except in Europe, Brazil and the Philippines) was in the region of twenty and captive breeding had occurred, but some years previously, and possibly in only one collection.

Its extreme rarity, making it the most expensive parrot in existence, may result in its extinction. A Brazilian trapper can earn more from catching and selling one bird than in a decade or more of working. It is a tragic state of affairs for which there seems to be no answer at present.

In 1987, the very few holders of this species outside Brazil agreed to co-operate in pairing and lending birds. There is a good chance that captive breeding will occur outside Brazil and no reason to suppose that this species would be especially difficult. The problem is that very few birds are available and they are scattered so widely throughout the world.

SPRAYING

Although bathing facilities are provided for birds which do not have access to rain, these are generally insufficient to ensure good condition of the plumage. Small birds may be able to bathe in the water container provided, but a thorough bath will be impossible for larger species. They can be seen dipping their heads in the water – sometimes obviously longing for a thorough soaking. This is best achieved by means of spraying. Buy a plant mister for a small number of birds, or a large pressure spray for many. It is hard work using a hand spray if thirty or more need a soaking!

If spraying with warm water is a new experience, birds may object at first, and a light spray only is advisable. However, they soon learn to love it and become excited, ruffling their feathers, and perhaps anticipating the water by ducking their heads in the water pot, at the first glimpse of the spray. No conscientious owner will neglect this aspect of care; the birds derive so much enjoyment from it and their plumage acquires a wonderful gloss.

When drenched with water, the

plumage takes on a leaden appearance in many birds. In those in which it is in excellent condition, perhaps after years of spraying, the water may just roll off, hardly seeming to penetrate the feathers or change their colour. Moisture is essential if plumage is not to become dry and brittle; it also encourages a bird to preen vigorously.

In warm weather, it is best to spray a bird outside, leaving it inside its cage if not tame or wing-clipped. Alternatively, the base of the cage can be removed and spraying carried out over a sink. The cage can then be cleaned, to ensure there is no accumulation of feather dust.

STRESS

'Stress is the biggest killer of cage birds' wrote a British veterinarian some years ago, before most of us were aware of how true this is. Stress kills birds which are not 100% fit but which, quite possibly, would live for years with some disease or condition which, under optimum conditions, could be tolerated.

One of the advantages of hand-rearing is that it produces very tame birds, and such birds are not easily stressed. In contrast, wild-taken adult birds are extremely nervous and quickly stressed by close confinement or close contact with humans. There are no figures to substantiate this, but I would guess that the life-span of a tame parrot averages two or three times more, at the very least, than that of a nervous bird. Tame birds recover much more quickly from accidents or other traumatic experiences. They suffer little or no shock from being caught or handled and, when they are breeding, inspecting their nests is more likely to produce aggression than a nervous reaction.

Other factors being equal, some species are much more susceptible to stress than others. As a very general observation, Amazons are not easily stressed, but Grey Parrots and cockatoos are. Nearly all cases of feather plucking are due to some form of stress. This is rarely seen in Amazons, but is very common in Greys and fairly common in cockatoos.

In some very rare cases, stress may have a genetic basis, perhaps due to in-breeding. I know of two examples in parrots which come from extremely small islands where continuous in-breeding has almost certainly occurred. The Uvaean Parrakeet (see under *Eunymphicus PARRAKEETS*) is very susceptible to stress, unlike the closely related Horned Parrakeet. The habitat of the Uvaean is an area only 4 or 5 km (2½–3 miles) in extent.

The most easily stressed species that I have bred is the Tahiti Blue Lory (*Vini peruviana*), which also occurs on very small islands with very small populations. Regrettably, I have had numerous tragic experiences with such birds which I had hand-reared and which were, therefore, very tame. Usually, as the result of quarrelling with another bird (although there were no injuries, or no significant injuries), a Blue Lory would be so stressed it would become comatose within minutes.

Only in a couple of instances was a bird revived. In one case, massaging the heart saved it; in another case, stimulating the heart with drugs given orally (not injected) failed to save its life.

So often birdkeepers subject their pets or aviary inhabitants to unnecessary stress when a little thought could avoid such situations. When catching birds in an aviary, for example, do so in a place (shelter or flight) where as few other birds as possible will be disturbed. Do not worm a bird immediately after it has been caught – perhaps having been chased for two or three minutes. Put it in a cage and wait until it has quietened down and its breathing has returned to normal. Do not go along a range of aviaries worming the occupants if all the birds in the range can see what is happening. They will all be in a stressed condition as a result of watching other birds being caught.

Avoid sudden or loud noises. Do not startle your parrots by appearing without warning if they are unable to see your approach. Give some 'contact call', such as a whistle or a word of greeting. Remember that any new or strange objects, even different clothing, can cause alarm, especially to nervous young birds which have not long left the nest.

T and U

SWIFT PARRAKEET (*Lathamus discolor*)

The only member of its genus, this is a most distinctive little parrakeet, unlike any other in appearance and behaviour. Its small beak, gentle and dainty appearance and most attractive song (this word is an exaggeration in almost all other parrots except the Purple-bellied, *Triclaria*) are especially pleasing.

It originates from Australia, where flowering trees are its main source of food. Like lories, Swift Parrakeets feed extensively on pollen and nectar, and have a brush tongue for gathering pollen. A varied diet is recommended, such as that provided by the German aviculturist, the late Josef Schumacher. He fed his Swifts on apple, orange and soft fruits in season, such as strawberries, sprouted sunflower, millet, oat, wheat, hemp and niger, half-ripened wheat (stored in a freezer for year-round use), corn on the cob and sponge cake moistened with honey.

Australian aviculturists are able to supply fresh branches of gum, such as peppermint or white gum, in which the birds enjoy bathing when the branches are wet. They also relish flowers, such as fuchsia, which contain nectar. The Swifts at Loro Parque greatly enjoy nibbling at the pine branches with which they are supplied regularly.

As aviary birds, Swift Parrakeets can be highly recommended. They have delightful voices – incapable of being loud – they are not destructive, and they nest fairly readily. Three to five eggs are laid and incubated by the female for about twenty days. The young spend about five weeks in the nest. On fledging they are extremely pretty, with softer colours than their parents, dark eyes and shorter tails. Bread and milk is a good rearing food for this species.

In the wild the species breeds only in the east and central part of Tasmania. After breeding they disperse to the western part of the island, and then, in the autumn, most of the population migrates to the mainland. This species is gregarious even when breeding (more than one nest may be found in the same tree) and out of the breeding season it is found in flocks.

Tanygnathus PARROTS

Five members of this genus have been named; the authenticity of one is doubtful, another (*gramineus*) is unknown in captivity at the time of writing, and the other three are interesting and very under-rated in aviculture. Originating from Indonesia and the Philippines, they have not been frequently exported and comparatively little has been recorded about them as aviary birds. They range in size from about 31 to 41 cm (12–16 in) and have fairly broad tails of short to medium length.

These parrots accept a wide variety of foods. All the usual seeds, fruits and vegetables, including corn on the cob, should be offered.

The most imposing is the Great-billed Parrot (*T. megalorynchos*), notable for its huge bill and for the beauty of its wing markings. The bill is generally slightly larger in the male; there is no difference in the plumage. Widely distributed throughout Indonesia, there are eight sub-species with slight plumage differences. Immature birds have narrower and paler yellow margins on the wing coverts.

Quiet in behaviour and voice, the Great-bill is unlikely to have a wide appeal. However, tame birds are delightful. A friendly male at Loro Parque attracts one's attention not by vocalisation, but by bobbing up and down. He was received in November 1987, at which time there was no report of this species having bred in captivity, and nothing had been recorded of its breeding habits in the wild. In January 1988, the female laid two eggs. This clutch was infertile, but from a second clutch of three laid in March, two chicks hatched.

A smaller version of the Great-bill, with almost similar wing markings and soft blue on the crown, is the Blue-naped Parrot (*T. lucionensis*) from the Philippines and Indonesia. Its length is about 31 cm (12 in). Males are usually more brightly coloured, especially on the wings.

This species is not well known in aviculture, but a few breeding successes have occurred. The two eggs are incubated for twenty-six days by the female. The young remain in the nest for approximately eight weeks. Gentle, quiet and pretty, they are most attractive aviary birds.

Adults of Müller's Parrot (*T. sumatranus* or *T. mulleri*) are very easy to sex: the beak is red in the male and white in the female, and also in immature birds. It differs from the Blue-naped Parrot mainly in lacking blue on the head. It, too, originates from the Philippines and from Indonesia.

TEACHING PARROTS TO TALK

Many people are attracted to the idea of having a parrot which can 'talk', that is, mimic. Many parrots will even say the right phrase at the right time – by association. For example, when someone is making preparations to go out, the bird will say 'bye bye', but parrots cannot normally be credited with actually knowing what they are saying.

To produce a good mimic, the three most important factors are a young bird, a suitable species, and a teacher who has patience. It is usually necessary to have a tame bird, or at least one which has accepted close confinement. An unhappy, nervous bird is very unlikely to mimic speech.

Although many species of parrots will learn to repeat half a dozen words, there are relatively few species that can acquire a sizeable vocabulary. These are Grey Parrots, certain species of Amazons, Eclectus and some of the larger lories.

Incidentally, parrots can learn to 'talk' from listening to other parrots, but usually the teacher is a human friend. To start with, choose a short, simple phrase such as 'hello', 'bye bye' or 'come on'. Repeat it at least three or four times whenever you pass the parrot's cage. In addition, have two ten-minute sessions of repeating the phrase when there are no competing distractions, such as television, and the room is fairly quiet.

Most parrots are not capable of mimicking different voices but 'speak' in the same voice, regardless of who has taught them. Greys and some Amazons are an exception and some of these birds are capable of reproducing the voices of several different people. Just as in the human child, the age at which they commence to mimic, and the length of time it takes to learn words, vary greatly from individual to individual. Some hand-reared parrots commence at an extraordinarily early age – even before they are weaned (small macaws, for example) – yet other hand-reared birds, even Greys, may not utter a word before they are nine months old. Parrots are capable of remembering phrases for years without repeating them, then something will prompt their memory, such as the sudden appearance of a former owner, and they start to use them again.

Tepui **PARROTLET** – see *Nannopsittaca* **PARROTLETS**

It is not generally known that the larger lories, such as this Black-winged, are often excellent mimics.

138

Touit PARROTLETS

These small parrots, which measure from 14–17 cm (5½–7 in), are virtually unknown in aviculture. There are two reasons for this: they inhabit the forest canopy and are therefore difficult to locate, and the few birds which have been caught have proved extremely difficult to adapt to captivity. They originate from South America, and also Costa Rica in Central America.

They have a stocky build and short, slightly rounded tails. The beak is prominent, stout and strongly curved. Most are sexually dimorphic, the females being less colourful on the wings and tails.

Very little is known about these birds in the wild, but their unusual beak may indicate specialised feeding habits, thus explaining why the few attempts to keep these birds in captivity have not been successful. Possibly only the Lilac-tailed (*T. batavica*) has been kept outside its country of origin.

Herbert Murray, from Essex, England, twice imported this species from Trinidad. On the second occasion, he received two adults and two young ones (caught together in a net at night). They had been force-fed in Trinidad. They would not eat seed, fruit or mealworms, but existed on nectar plus a proprietary food for birds. When the manufacturers ceased to make this and another kind was used, three of the birds died.

This species is extremely beautiful, with colourful and unusually marked plumage. The forehead is yellow, the crown green, the nape feathers greenish-yellow tipped with black, the back brownish-black and the wings, tail coverts and rump are black. The tail is striking, the central feathers being violet and outer feathers mauvish-violet barred with black near the tip.

Food in the wild is known to include fruits, nectar, berries, seeds and buds.

So little is known about the *Touit* parrotlets that immature plumage has never been described in some of the seven species.

One, the Golden-tailed (*T. surda*), from eastern Brazil, is endangered by deforestation. Another, a mountain-dwelling species from south-western Colombia, northern Peru and eastern Ecuador, has seldom been observed. This is the Spot-winged Parrotlet (*T. stictoptera*), usually found at elevations of 1,400–2,000 m (4,600–6,560 ft).

Trichoglossus LORIKEETS

Most of the lorikeets in this genus are medium-sized with longish tails, but several are small with proportionately shorter tails. Nearly all have barred markings on the upper breast. They originate from Australia, New Guinea, New Caledonia and Indonesia. Some species occur in very large flocks.

In addition to nectar, fruit and greenfood, most *Trichoglossus* enjoy seed, such as canary and soaked sunflower. The amount should be greatly increased when young are being reared. One species, the Iris (*T. iris*), which is rare in captivity, needs a diet consisting of at least 50% seed and cannot live on nectar alone as the other species could.

Generally speaking, the members of this genus breed well in captivity and will rear several broods in one year; eight or ten youngsters in a year is not exceptional, although the clutch consists of only two eggs. The exception is the Perfect Lorikeet (*T. euteles*) which lays three eggs, or four on rare occasions.

The incubation period is twenty-three or twenty-four days and the young spend between seven and eight weeks in the nest. The smaller species will breed in a cage. One of the smallest, Goldie's (*T. goldiei*) actually breeds better in a cage than in an aviary. It is quiet, very pretty and not destructive – in fact, the perfect bird for anyone attracted to lories but unable to erect outdoor aviaries.

One of the most prolific species is the Green-naped (*T. haematodus haematodus*), a very colourful bird and readily available at a reasonable price. It has more than twenty sub-species whose identification can be difficult. Descriptions would be tedious as the plumage is intricate and the differences subtle. Among the best known are Edwards's (*T. h. capistratus*), which has the breast mainly yellow, Massena's (*T. h. massena*), which has the nape brown, and Swainson's or the Blue Mountain Lorikeet (*T. h. moluccanus*) from Australia, which is surely the most beautiful.

VASA PARROTS (*Coracopsis*)

The two species of Vasas are totally unlike any other parrots in appearance and behaviour. They are almost certainly the most primitive of parrots. Indeed, after studying them closely for three years (including the development of the young of *C. nigra*), I believe that they are the link between the parrots and the pigeons. (The latter family are generally accepted as being the nearest relatives of the parrots.)

They sun-bathe like pigeons, their feathers are similar and the young have very soft plumage; were it not for the shape of the beak they could be mistaken for young pigeons. The Lesser Vasa (*C. nigra*) has the extraordinarily short incubation period of fourteen days – significantly shorter than any other parrot. No other true parrot develops so rapidly and leaves the nest so early – at about five weeks. At the time of writing, there was no published report of the Greater Vasa (*C. vasa*) ever having been bred in captivity.

Some aspects of their behaviour, however, are unlike both pigeons *and* parrots. For example, the male has a loud and attractive whistling song. In the Greater *both* sexes protrude the sexual organs several centimetres when in breeding condition, the feathers on the top of the head are lost and the skin turns yellow – really bright yellow in some birds. The normally grey plumage becomes darker in some birds in breeding condition and the beak colour changes from grey to a pale horn colour.

So much remains to be learned about this behaviourally fascinating genus. Their dull grey plumage will attract no one, but their pleasing personalities and unique behaviour will appeal to the discerning – and the conservation-conscious – aviculturist. They are found in Madagascar and the Comoro Islands, and the Lesser has a sub-species on Praslin, a very small island in the Seychelles.

Hundreds of Vasas have been exported from Madagascar since the early 1980s, because of the very severe destruction of habitat which is occurring there. Vasas will almost certainly be classified as endangered within a decade, so it behoves serious aviculturists to ensure that they are established in captivity before it is too late.

Immature birds resemble adults except that the beak is dark.

The length is about 50 cm (20 in) in the Greater, and about 38 cm (15 in) in the Lesser.

Vasas are hardy and easy to feed. They will accept a very wide range of items. Some show a preference for small seeds (a mixture should be provided) including spray millet, and walnuts and pine nuts are relished. A wide variety of vegetables, greenfoods and fruits should be offered.

VEGETABLES

Vegetables suitable for parrots can be divided into three categories: leaf, root and other (such as tomato). A wide variety of leaf vegetables are acceptable, especially spinach, kale and lettuce. Some of the larger species will eat the leaves and stems of

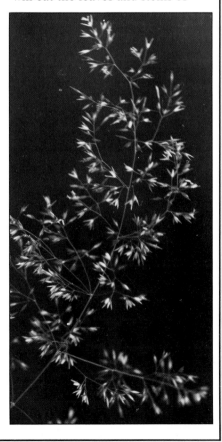

Annual meadow grass (*Poa annua*).

cabbage, cauliflower and also broccoli.

Among the most suitable leafy weeds are sowthistle, chickweed and young dandelion leaves. Great care must be exercised to obtain these from areas where spraying of pesticides has not occurred. No more should be offered than can be consumed in a few hours, as, unless placed in a container of water, greenfoods soon become limp and unappetising. Many kinds of grasses, such as annual meadow grass (*Poa annua*) and wheat are relished by a wide variety of species. Watercress is excellent. The owner of a single bird can keep a bunch of watercress for two or three days in a glass of water.

The most important root vegetable is carrot, which can be diced for smaller species and offered in larger pieces to the bigger birds. Some will not eat it unless it is placed firmly between the wires of the cage or aviary. Raw carrot is valuable for its Vitamin A content. Beetroot will be eaten by some parrots, especially if they start to receive it when young.

Other suitable vegetables are celery, tomato, courgettes and red and green peppers. Fresh corn on the cob is a universal favourite. In countries where the growing season is short, it is advisable to buy cobs in quantity when available, blanch them (place them in boiling water for one minute), and then freeze them for use throughout the year. (Bought frozen cobs are expensive.) Cooking is not required, only thawing. Some small species, including lories, also relish the sweetcorn kernels, which can be obtained tinned or frozen. Apart from corn, only fresh vegetables are recommended. Peas in the pod and green beans are also very popular.

VETERINARY ADVICE AND CARE

Birdkeepers should not wait until they have a sick bird, which urgently needs expert attention, to search for a veterinarian in their area, who is experienced in handling cage birds, especially parrots. In the USA, especially in California and Florida, avian veterinary specialists can be found. Elsewhere it can be very difficult indeed to find a veterinarian with any experience or knowledge of parrots. Local breeders, a local bird society or even a pet shop may be able to recommend a suitable vet. It is worth contacting him or her in advance, stating that you keep parrots and may need advice in the future.

Do not fail to seek veterinary advice just because you are unable to find an avian specialist. Remember that all vets have laboratory services available to them. Faecal analysis usually provides useful information regarding a sick bird; the main problem is that it is relatively slow. It could be forty-eight hours or more before laboratory results are obtained and an untreated sick bird is likely to die within this period. A parrot's metabolism is very rapid (the smaller the bird, the more rapid it is) and heat, and usually treatment, must commence immediately once it is noticed that a bird is unwell.

Vini LORIES

Small lories of extraordinary appeal and beauty, there are five species of *Vini* which are virtually unknown in captivity. They originate from remote islands of the South Pacific and also Fiji. Their size is in the region of 18 cm (7 in), and their plumage is mainly green or mainly blue, with shaft-streaking on the head feathers. Male and female are alike.

The *Vini* lories do best in planted, slightly heated enclosures. They do not easily tolerate low temperatures. Their diet consists principally of nectar and also fruit, especially pomegranates, grapes, apple and pear.

The clutch consists of two eggs which are incubated by both male and female for twenty-five days.

The Tahiti Blue lory (*V. peruviana*) is an exquisite little creature. It is a glossy violet-blue, with the lower face and upper breast white. The orange bill and legs provide a striking contrast. Adult plumage is obtained at about six months, before which young birds are dark greyish-blue, with face and breast greyish-white and the beak brownish. This species is currently kept and bred in only two collections worldwide. (See *STRESS*.)

WATER

Parrots must have drinking water available at all times, and this must be provided fresh daily. The water container must also be cleaned daily or the water will become contaminated by the deposits in the container. Many parrots will bathe in standing water, so this fact should be borne in mind when choosing the water receptacle. For the most enthusiastic bathers, such as conures, it is advisable to have a small dish of water for drinking (they will dip their heads in almost any container) and a larger, shallower one for bathing. Lories are equally enthusiastic bathers.

A few species (such as cockatoos) do not normally bathe in standing water, but they delight in rain bathing. In areas of meagre or infrequent rainfall, aviaries should be fitted with sprinklers (obtainable at garden centres for use in greenhouses).

Careful thought should be given to the choice and location of water containers. Plastic hook-on pots are suitable for small parrots, and these can be placed at perch level or on a feeding shelf at a similar height. Heavy earthenware pots (such as dog bowls) are suitable for large or mischievous birds which delight in playing with anything movable. These can be placed on the floor (well away from perches where they would be contaminated with droppings) or on the feeding shelf. Cat litter trays make useful water containers in an aviary containing a number of birds.

Adopt a routine for dealing with water containers during freezing weather. Empty the water pots at dusk; it is a lot easier than thawing out solid ice next morning. Water can be prevented from freezing during the day by standing the container on bricks and placing a night light candle (the short, wide type), well hidden, beneath the container. However, this is only practical where a small number of containers are involved.

Automatic watering systems are available in the USA and are gradually being offered for sale in other countries. They are very useful for large establishments where changing and cleaning water containers is a time-consuming task. Different types of watering systems have been marketed. One of them, to give an example, depends on a pivoting stem drinking valve. The valve has a protruding stem which is deflected when the bird touches it with tongue or beak, resulting in a flow of water. This ceases when the stem is released. The small quantity of water at the end of the stem attracts the bird. Because domestic water supplies have a higher pressure than that used in this system, a storage tank must be used. It cannot operate from tap water.

WINTER CARE

Special attention must be paid to the welfare of birds kept in outdoor aviaries during the winter. In cold climates there will be deaths, which could easily have been avoided, unless certain precautions are taken. Most parrots tolerate low temperatures quite well, but the combination of cold and wet conditions is unacceptable for many species, especially *Neophemas* and other small species which do not use their nest-boxes for roosting. They are best housed indoors or in a birdroom during the colder months.

Electric lighting is very important; small birds need to be able to feed for at least twelve hours each day. The energy obtained from the food helps them to maintain their body temperature in cold weather, and thus lighting is actually more important than heating. However, infra-red lamps in the shelter will be appreciated by many species (see *INFRA-RED LAMP*).

Aviaries should be protected from wind. The best method is to erect polythene or plastic-covered frames around the enclosures. Draughts can literally be lethal. I was told of a pair of lories, roosting in a shelter with moderate heat, which were found dead, frozen to the perch, after an exceptionally cold night. The entrance hole to the shelter had not been closed and the lories had roosted in line with an icy blast.

Another winter problem is frost-bite. Certain species (such as *Psittacula* parrakeets and lovebirds) are especially susceptible. Birds which roost in the nest-box will not be affected.

Psittacula parrakeets such as this male Derbyan are extremely susceptible to frost-bite.

Extra wide wooden perches can be an advantage, as they push the birds' toes forward to be covered by the breast feathers. After a frosty night, perches must be checked carefully for signs of blood. Birds with frozen toes may bite them off, having lost all sensation in their feet. Their toes or nails must immediately be cauterised to stop further bleeding. (The surgical cautery for birds, sold by Phoenix Unlimited in the USA, is highly recommended for this purpose.) Swelling of the feet is sometimes an indication that frost-bite will occur if a bird is left out of doors any longer. If serious swelling occurs, consult a veterinarian, as a cortisone injection may be necessary.

All birds kept in outdoor aviaries should be inspected daily just prior to dusk. A bird which is sick, or behaving uncharacteristically, may be observed and should be put in a warm place for the night. A sick bird would be unable to survive several hours of low temperatures. If you are unable to inspect your birds (including chicks in the nest) at first light and just before they go to roost, do not keep them in outdoor aviaries. Keep them indoors or in an electrically lit outdoor birdroom – or not at all!

WORMING

Some species are extremely susceptible to intestinal worms, the most common being *Ascaridia*. The most likely birds to be affected are Australian parrakeets, cockatiels, lovebirds and Kakarikis. These are all birds which like to search around on the aviary floor where they may encounter the eggs of parasitic worms, from wild birds or other aviary occupants. If these are ingested, they will hatch in the bird's digestive system and grow in the intestines, feeding on the contents and depriving the bird of nourishment.

A low level of worm infestation could be tolerated for a long period, but the danger is that the worms will increase to the point where their host becomes thin and weak and the intestines are blocked or ruptured. The bird will die unless treatment is given before this stage is reached. It should be carried out at least twice yearly, before and after the breeding season. Even young birds can be badly affected, worm eggs having been passed to them in food from their parents.

A number of preparations are available which can be used for worming parrakeets, most of which were formulated for agricultural use, for far larger animals. Some veterinarians can advise on a safe dosage for parrakeets and show the best method of administering it. If a veterinarian is unable to do this, advice should be sought from an experienced breeder, because administering it directly into the crop is the only efficient method.

Most worming preparations have a bitter taste, so that adding them to the drinking water is not effective; some birds will accept them if added to a favourite softfood. This is a hit and miss method, but it is perfectly safe.

It has to be admitted that many birds have died as a result of administering the preparation directly into the crop, either from shock or because the tube attached to the syringe has entered the windpipe instead of the crop.

The alternative to worming all parrakeets routinely, is to send their faecal samples to a laboratory and then treat only those which are found to have worm eggs in their faeces. This would be quite an expensive process, however. After a bird has been treated, the owner needs to know whether any worms are passed. This will be impossible unless the bird is caught and placed in a cage. The base should be lined with paper and the faeces examined during the following four to twenty-four hours. Treatment must be repeated within the next two or three weeks if worms are passed.

XYZ

ZOONOSES

Zoonoses, or zoonotic diseases, are diseases of animals which can be transferred to humans. There are apparently over 100 diseases of animals which fall into this category, but it is chlamydiosis which receives so much adverse publicity for birds in the press. This disease, and Newcastle, are the most important zoonotic diseases of birds. The latter may be found in poultry pathologists or laboratory workers. Symptoms are severe conjunctivitis or sinusitis.

Chlamydiosis is also known as psittacosis when found in parrots, and ornithosis in other birds. It is common in pigeons. In fact, a tourist feeding a flock of pigeons in Trafalgar Square, or some other popular location, is more likely to be affected than the owner of a single parrot. Newly imported parrots, even although they have been quarantined, present some disease risk, but the organism is also fairly common in budgies, and finches and canaries can also transmit chlamydia. The danger to parrot keepers, although real, has therefore been exaggerated.

Chlamydia is caused by an organism related to bacteria, *Chlamydia psittaci*. Faeces are a source of the organism, which could be digested by other birds as a result of eating the faeces, or inhaled into the respiratory system. Whichever route is taken, when the *Chlamydia* bacteria reach the liver and spleen, they multiply. Symptoms in birds may include a discharge from eyes and nostrils, weight loss and possibly diarrhoea. The carrier of the disease may show no symptoms, but could infect many other birds.

If a possible diagnosis of chlamydia has been made, it is suggested that all birds which have been in contact with affected birds should be treated with antibiotics. Unfortunately, the treatment is very long, taking at least two months. It must, of course, be carried out under veterinary supervision.

In people, the incubation period of the disease usually ranges from five days to two weeks. Symptoms include fever, muscular aches and respiratory problems; an infected person may believe that he or she is suffering from influenza. The main danger is that chlamydiosis will not be diagnosed and the patient will not be correctly treated. If the condition is diagnosed immediately, it will clear up in a few days with the use of tetracycline.